Praise for
Finding Myself

"An inspiring book about facing obstacles, building strength, and achieving excellence. Crystal Robinson is not just a great basketball player—she's also a powerful writer."

ADAM GRANT,
New York Times #1 Bestselling Author, *Think Again*,
Host of the TED Podcast WorkLife

"Crystal is a truly resilient and empowering role model for all the young women out there. A true inspiration."

JACK CANFIELD,
Co-founder, Chicken Soup for the Soul ®
New York Times #1 Bestseller, *The Success Principles* ™

"Crystal went from being a young girl in Oklahoma growing up in poverty, to being a Basketball Hall of Famer. How did she achieve such a feat? She persevered. She gave herself permission to be great. And most of all, she refused to let her circumstances hold her back. We could all benefit from taking a page from Crystal's book. Alternating between stories of tragedy, and undeniably funny scenes, you feel like you're right there with her the whole time. She will become your friend and confidante, and the whole time, you can't help but root for her."

PATTY AUBERY,
Founder, Permission Granted ™
New York Times #1 Bestseller, *Chicken Soup for the Christian Soul* ®

"In *Finding Myself*, Crystal Robinson reveals the surprising strength and resiliency that powered her success on the court, but ultimately teaches us these same traits can empower us in our own striving."

DEENA KASTOR,
Olympic medalist and American record holder, marathon,
New York Times bestselling author, *Let Your Mind Run*

"Sometimes life takes us down the road less traveled. But often times when that happens, despite the hardships, it allows us to find ourselves. And as a result, we become more tolerant, understanding, empathetic, nurturing, and compassionate people. Crystal epitomizes that and her contagious spirit, energy, and staying true to her inner voice continues to allow her to inspire and lead others. And because Crystal has such a genuine understanding of herself, it has allowed her to heal, evolve, and be in spaces she never thought possible as a kid. She's a true hero and it's been an honor to cross paths with her. *Finding Myself* will inspire people to find themselves and realize they are not alone."

MICHAEL HOOTNER,
Host of *The Sports Deli* podcast

"As the late, great coach Don Meyer once said, "It's not your advice, it's your example." And what an amazing example Crystal Robinson has set in her life through all her trials and tribulations. It is hard to imagine at times that someone can find peace and success with so many roadblocks but to be resilient and to persevere through her difficulties powerfully comes off the pages and serves as proof that we too can conquer our hardships. Thanks Crystal – not just for the courage you have shown to overcome adversity but for your courage to share your story so that it might inspire others to do the same."

BOB STARKEY,
Assistant coach, women's basketball, Texas A&M University

"*Finding Myself* was awe-inspiring and a powerful story from cover to cover. Crystal's basketball accolades and fame may have been known to many but her resolve and perseverance through her internal battles should be most applauded. This autobiography has the ability to provide the hope that we need in today's climate. Thank you Crystal for your vulnerability and exceptional story telling!"

SHARNEE ZOLL-NORMAN,
Assistant coach, women's basketball, University of Rhode Island

"Crystal Robinson is a name that is well known by Oklahomans and synonymous with the word winner in that state. I had the good fortune of watching Crystal in person for years and always admired her mental toughness and competitive greatness. I followed her professional career closely and watched as she turned herself into an iconic professional player. Crystal understands the concept of team and was a highly intelligent player who saw the game at a different level than many of her contemporaries. *Finding Myself* is a must-read in which we are given an in-depth look at the path that led Crystal to develop the type of heart she exhibited on the court. I admire the courage, perseverance, and toughness she has forged into her character and applied to her professional career. I only hope that my own daughters can have the type of integrity, loyalty, and transparency that Crystal has demonstrated for a quarter century at the top of the sports industry."

JOHN MARCUM,
Assistant coach, women's basketball, Syracuse University

"When I first came into the WNBA, Crystal was basically the team mom. Her passion for the game, her enthusiasm for life, and her dedication to being the best version of herself are the things that I remember most. We all have struggles and we all have joys. With everything that life hands her, Crystal chooses JOY! Outsiders would see two people from opposite sides of the track, but basketball and faith are two of the links that bound us. I learned just as much from observing Crystal off the court as I did working beside her on it. I can't think of my time in the WNBA without thinking of the amazing teammates and friendships formed. This book is a reminder to us all that hardships can be good, struggles help us grow, and hard work makes winners of us all. As C-Rob says, we get to choose the memories that mold us and I am grateful that some of my most precious memories included her!"

ERIN THORN,
Basketball player, Tarbes GB

"I had the great fortune to coach Crystal Robinson from 1999 to 2004 when I was the Head Coach of the WNBA's New York Liberty. Crystal Robinson's superb defense and clutch shooting when the game was on the line is only part of what makes her an incredible woman. Her kindness of heart, determination and resilience make her a true role model. Her legacy will endure as one of strength, hope and infinite compassion. *Finding Myself* is a coming of age memoir of poignant glimpses into her incredible life, showing mistakes made and lessons learned. The three Eastern Conference Championship banners in the rafters of Madison Square Garden are a testament to Crystal's talent and hard work. I'm forever grateful to have coached her but more importantly, to call her my friend."

RICHIE ADUBATO,
Former NBA and WNBA head coach

"Having known Crystal for years and having heard bits and pieces of her life it was fascinating to learn how all the pieces fit together to make Crystal who she is today. Crystal is part of our family and it amazes me how much she has come through to become the person we have always known. We love her! Hopefully this book will lead others to never give up and keep their eyes on the prize."

JUDY FISCHMAN,
Retired teacher of forty-two years,
Chairman of Bloomfield Juvenile Conference Committee

"I had the pleasure of meeting C-Rob and playing for her for one year while I was in Dallas and I really enjoyed getting to know her then. After reading her book, I feel like I know her even better. I appreciate her being so open about her life and sharing all of the lessons that she has learned. Her book provides deep insight and wisdom about life, basketball and everything in between. I'm grateful to know someone like her and am inspired by her perseverance, humility and loving spirit."

AZURA STEVENS,
WNBA player, Chicago Sky

"Passionate, tenacious, and authentic describe how Crystal lives her life and shares her story in *Finding Myself*, with courage and commitment to enrich and encourage others—particularly those of us who have known struggles and have had to make our own path in life. I remember meeting C-Rob about twenty years ago when I walked into the team practice at Chelsea Piers in New York City. I remember her saying, 'What's up, rookie?' and going out of her way to make small talk as I stood on the sidelines, anxious and nervous. During the two hours that followed our brief introduction and the following years of playing together, Crystal was a leader on and off the court, who led with a quiet strength, poise, and unmatched sense of humor that helped defy any challenge or adversity that we faced as a team. Crystal was never one who sought the spotlight, but she always attracted others with her humility, kindness, strong work ethic, and free spirit. Crystal was certainly 'the glue,' the prankster, and deft shooter whose person off the court spoke louder than her game on the court. *Finding Myself* is a story of triumph, trials, tragedy, and success—and behind every three-point goal, every drive to the basic, and every win that she helped lead us to was the story of a woman who had already won and overcame so many obstacles in life. Crystal is a true champion who has overcome the odds and set the bar high for all who are blessed to call her a friend, family, coach, or to simply be in her presence. Crystal, thank you for sharing your story, and I am honored to call you my teammate and friend."

CAMILLE COOPER,
Former WNBA player, New York Liberty

"Crystal Robinson's story of triumph over and through adversity is truly amazing! Knowing how much she overcame to ascend to the tallest heights in our profession is truly inspiring. A must-read for anyone who desires to see a modern-day example of resilience in action."

COQUESE WASHINGTON,
Associate head coach, women's basketball, University of Notre Dame

"Crystal was a fierce competitor and an unbelievable player with an absolute heart of gold. Although we were often competitors in the WNBA, I always respected her sportsmanship, positivity, and most of all, her spirit and joy whenever our paths crossed. I had no idea about the life circumstances, obstacles and battles Crystal faced. This is a fantastic book for all those who need inspiration on how to cope, deal with and rise above adversity. It truly made me respect and admire Crystal even more!"

TAMMI REISS,
Head coach, women's basketball, University of Rhode Island

"I coached at Campbellsville University for thirty-two years and my teams had the opportunity to play against her at Southeastern Oklahoma. She could dominate a game. During one timeout she told
her team she was going to have to score sixty for them to win and she did. I followed her pro career in New York, then lost track of her."

DONNA WISE,
Head coach, women's basketball, Campbellsville University
Chairman of Human Performance

"Crystal shared her book with me in the early stages. I ended up almost reading it in its entirety in one sitting. Crystal has always been a person who shies away from any form of attention so I was excited to learn that she would have a platform to share her story. Through the years, I have heard of some of her childhood adventures and experiences. However, after reading her book I am in awe of the perseverance she has shown throughout her life. I look forward to Crystal's next chapter in life."

LISA FISCHMAN,
Maccabi USA Gold Medalist, Professional Basketball, Israel,
School Administrator and Athletic Director, Morristown, NJ

"I know Crystal as the special person she is, not the pro athlete or Hall-of-Famer or even celebrity. I met Crystal post her retirement. When I met her, she was just a regular person. She has this fun, loving way about her. She doesn't seem to take herself too seriously. You can tell she loves strong and her family is everything to her. You can see that when she looks at her sister or at her nephew, even when teasing or making jokes with or about them. She would joke about little things growing up, like killing and eating squirrels, or when she did something crazy and got a whipping from her mama. Reading about her life, how she overcame such struggles, challenges and just plain horrible situations makes me love and respect her even more. Look at the beautiful person Crystal is. I feel blessed to call Crystal Robinson my friend."

MICHELLE LEONARDIS,
Certified Personal Trainer, Senior Health Investigator, Bloomfield, NJ

"It's not very often in life you come across a person with such a successful career and yet is so humble you would never know it. Crystal is a person that exemplifies the saying 'what you see is what you get.' She never lets her success get to her head and change her as a person. By reading her book you know where she got her work ethic and calm demeanor. Having known Crystal for quite some time now, I knew some of the stories but learned so much more after completing this wonderful portrayal of her life. Now having a better grasp of her past and knowing her today, I can't wait to see what the future holds for this incredible athlete, businesswoman, sister, daughter and most of all, friend. One thing is for sure, it's going to be an adventure!"

JILL FISCHMAN,
Educator of twenty-two years,
New Providence head softball coach,
Former collegiate basketball player and coach

Finding Myself

An autobiography by
CRYSTAL ROBINSON

Copyright © 2021 Crystal Robinson
Illustrations and cover design by Charlotte Pearce
Photography by Raw Images Photography
Interior design and typesetting by Paul Neuviale

Distribution by KDP Amazon and Ingram Spark (P.O.D.)

Printed in the United States of America
Title: Finding Myself
Author: Crystal Robinson

Hardcover ISBN: 978-1-7775737-2-0
Paperback ISBN: 978-1-7775737-0-6
Ebook ISBN: 978-1-7775737-1-3

Publisher: Talk+Tell

Book description: A memoir about Crystal Robinson, a retired WNBA
player and NAIA Hall-of-Famer and how she refused to let the world
bring her down.

This book is dedicated to my family.

Our story is filled with struggle, but it is equally filled with love, forgiveness and strength.

My life is something that can only be valued by really seeing my imperfections.

***

To Phil:

Life is about choosing which memories we allow to define us. I hope the readers of my book don't get caught up in the struggle but see all the beautiful blessings instead.

Thank you and Karen for choosing to see me as a person instead of a basketball player. Thank you for fighting for me when it wasn't the popular thing to do. Thank you for leaving me for being late to the bus like everyone else. Thank you for believing in me and standing with me always. Your legacy will be passed along for decades to come because I don't know a girl that played for you that doesn't feel the same way I do!

Since you're gone now, I guess I can reveal that you beat me in Horse more than anyone except for Laurie Koehn. You were smart enough to stop playing me! Anyone that knows me, knows that before the handicapped days, I was the Horse wrangler. Rest easy, Phil. I hope you'll see your influence between these lines.

Steel Rose presents Crystal Robinson!

A Conscious Sisterhood

Be seen, be heard... BELONG!

Lead with the strength of steel,
Live with the grace of a rose,
Love with dignity.

A private collective of conscious women who lead with love and dignity.

We turn mutual support into a competitive edge defined by team spirit and mutual success.

We are movers and shakers.

We are here to define a new status quo for love, giving, and decision-making.

We discover success in every aspect of our lives and environment.

Our sisterhood is full of women who have overcome significant life challenges and now choose the direction of love and co-creation. Together, we are on a mission to serve with certainty and purpose.

A TESTAMENT TO CRYSTAL'S STRENGTH AND LOVE

by SUSAN HUM, founder of Steel Rose

Crystal Robinson represents the epitome of the Steel Rose way. She has showcased strength and perseverance in the face of poverty, racism, and struggle. Crystal has used each challenge as a tool to stay focused on being a positive role model for any woman who chooses love and compassion. She is one of few people I know who can look beyond circumstances and appearances without judgment. Instead, Crystal looks straight into the heart while also looking beyond culture and skin color.

Since she was a child, she has held on to this philosophy of never wanting to judge people, even though she had every reason to do so. She chose never to impart the pain of rejection through racism and prejudice on anyone who crosses her path. She was looking for people's truth. And in truth lies true love. All she ever wanted was true love, from people, from a life partner, and today with Steel Rose, she found love with herself. Her story is proof of her accomplishments and why she is a Steel Rose.

Crystal's past experiences are what have made her a great role model and a real leader. She has shown endurance against adversity, has never cast herself in the role of a victim, and always sees the good in people. Crystal is a true Steel Rose, because she has fallen deeply in love with herself and is now able to attract true love to herself. And that is what a Steel Rose is – a woman who is so deeply in love with who she is and what she does, that she imparts that to anyone who crosses her path. That is the meaning of dignity.

ABOUT STEEL ROSE

Steel Rose is a movement for innovating love consciousness. It's a platform for all women to love themselves so they can be empowered to create the life of their dreams.

Our mission is to elevate love consciousness globally by narrowing all divides in society, whether between women, men and women, races or cultures, identity preferences, or personal beliefs. Love consciousness emerges from the ability to express our personal truth with freedom.

The Steel Rose way is defined by women who have overcome life's greatest challenges and emerge with the inner strength to thrive under any condition and environment. Together we are women who make a conscious choice to follow the direction of love and wellness to elevate ourselves and those around us. A Steel Rose can respond and no longer merely reacts.

We empower women of all cultures to unite and inspire and support one another to achieve their greatest dreams by leading with love, grace, and dignity. Together we are stronger.

https://www.susanhum.com/steel-rose-movement

Contents

"Before I ask you to sit with me, I must be able to sit with myself. Before I ask you to accept my pain, I have to accept the pain myself. Before I ask you to love me, I have to be madly in love with myself."

— *Unknown*

Foreword

I've known Crystal Robinson for many years; I watched her play in college. I watched her play in the WNBA. I saw the beauty of her game and the enormity of her team spirit. What a great ambassador of the game she was.

From afar, you could see this confident, effervescent, very quiet, but likable, young player, not yet fully understanding where she came from and the obstacles she had to rise above. When you read Crystal's book about her life, it's a book about overcoming any situation that society could put in front of her. It highlights her ability to shine in the face of adversity.

From family, to where she grew up, she was able to stay true to her past and focused on her dream. Going out, working on her game, making sure she was prepared for when her moment arrived.

It's never easy when you're young, and you have heart-breaking moments with your mom, or your dad, or the people around you. But that's where her heart and her love for God guided her, took her places that she never thought she might get to.

One of the constants in Crystal's life has been her fundamentals—fundamentals of life, fundamentals of friends, fundamentals of her belief.

I can remember how her teammates talked about her with reverence. She was never really the type of person to make excuses. It was always, "This is what we can do. This is how we're going to do it."

No matter what, people followed her quiet confidence. I think that's what drew me to Crystal; with all of the games and all of the athletes I've known over time, I recognized that her choices were different. How she carried herself set her apart from so many of the other players. She is a great woman, a great role model—never afraid, no matter what the situation.

Proud of her hometown, proud of her family, but always willing to prove to herself first that she could compete with anybody.

As we go through life and we get older, we recognize the fact that in our haste to gain rewards, sometimes we need to be able to stop and say, "I'm sorry, forgive me."

Saying that is one of the greatest things a person can do: to have that confidence and self-belief to look somebody in the eye and say, "I'm sorry."

Crystal does not have to say she's sorry. She played through her hurt. She played through her anger. She played through her angst. Never really letting people on the outside understand what she was going through on this adventure, her life's adventure, which she has so gracefully managed.

Well, now, she has had the opportunity to affect

other people's lives—day, after day, after day.

Crystal is a hometown hero—someone who set records across the board, realizing now that so many people had an imprint on her life. Her life will never be remembered on the number of points she scored or the threes hitting. She will be remembered as a team player first, a winner at every level she played.

Crystal Robinson came into the WNBA in 1999. She had the opportunity to play in the most famous arena in the world—Madison Square Garden. She was the sixth pick in the draft in 1999.

For seven years, she played for the New York Liberty. Crystal's career ended in 2006, and from there, the next step of her storied career took off. As an athlete, you have to be selfish. But as a coach, you have to have sympathy, compassion, and understanding for others. Crystal possessed all of those qualities and far more.

I am honored to be able to talk about my friend, Crystal Robinson. Her beliefs, who she was, where she came from, and the woman she has become.

Crystal Robinson—I'm so excited that God chose you.

As I tell my teams, expectations are always high. There are no excuses and no explanations, because if you're explaining your excuse, you don't want to assume accountability. Crystal, your whole life has been about accountability.

I never had the chance to get on the court to either play with or against you, but I did have the distinct pleasure of calling your games and seeing how you were a part of the change. This book should be in every young person's hands so they can see that adversity must be overcome and not used as a crutch—knowing that you had to experience some bumps in the road before you learned to have blind faith and trust in your journey. I'm excited about your book, I love your story, and I look forward to seeing how many lives you will change when people pick up your life's story.

God bless you.

— NANCY LIEBERMAN
mother of T. J. Cline,
Basketball-Hall-Of-Famer,
two-times Olympian

Introduction

*"Only a person who knows what it's like to
be defeated can reach down to the bottom of
their soul and come up with the extra ounce
of power it takes to win."*

— *Muhammad Ali*

If you are reading this book because you think it's about a basketball player, you are wrong. *Finding Myself* is about hope, struggle, and perseverance. Basketball is just the environment and setting.

Within these pages, you'll find a story about always striving for your best while accepting and growing from your failures. You'll read about dreams and fears and how to accept your reality even when no one else accepts it. Most importantly, this book is about how to relate to others' struggles and overcome obstacles.

Obstacles are placed in our paths to teach us the lessons we need to reach our full potential and become what we are destined to be. Sometimes these obstacles make us feel like we can't make it. I'm writing this book to tell you that you can.

As a little girl growing up in Stringtown, Oklahoma, never in my wildest dreams did I imagine I would be the first African American woman to be inducted into the Oklahoma Sports Hall of Fame. I remember first hearing about the news. I was at the banquet, sitting at a table surrounded by family and friends. I looked at each of their faces trying to imagine what they were feeling. My name was announced, and at that moment, I was inducted into the Oklahoma Sports Hall of Fame. Taking in this once-in-a-lifetime moment, I found myself experiencing a flurry of emotions. It was as if I were in a movie where time stopped, and the different memories of my life were ever so gently breezing through my mind, and I couldn't help but question how I arrived at this moment in my life.

As my emotions came over me in waves, I thought about game two of the 1999 WNBA finals. I was matched up against one of the best players in the league, Cynthia Cooper, and I was coming off of a poor game one performance. None of the experts gave me an inkling of a chance against Cooper in game two. Cynthia played for the Houston Comets. They boasted the big three, Cynthia Cooper, Sheryl Swoopes, and Tina Thompson. They were a match nightmare, to say the least, for every team in the WNBA. They had won all of the championships in the league up to this point. Everyone knew that to win a championship, you had to go through them. I was a very efficient professional athlete; however, they were better than us at almost every position. After scoring only one point in the first half, I came out and completely dominated the second half pouring in nineteen points. We won that game by one point on a Hail Mary at the buzzer. As soon as that shot went through the nets, everyone forgot I scored nineteen straight points.

The first-ever televised Kodak All-American Game also ran through my mind. It was another instance where I was being doubted and discredited by others. I remember the commentator saying, "Robinson can score thirty points a game in high school, but that's misleading because she plays six-on-six." That commentator said it as if I didn't even deserve to be there. But little did he know, I would be sure that no one was misled that night. When the final buzzer sounded, I had scored twenty-seven points and was named the Most Valuable Player of that game.

Even the newly formed American Basketball League crossed my mind. I was drafted into that league in the eighth round. The coach of my team and I were college rivals. She knew I could play, but I guess because we were an NAIA school, she questioned whether I could really compete at the upper echelon. I thought about the moment she pulled me to the side one day and told me that she knew I was a star at the NAIA level but hoped I could accept not being a key player and getting limited playing time. I went on to be named the Most Valuable Player of the American Basketball League that year.

All of these moments ran through my mind while

I sat with my family and friends. I experienced joy and pain, happiness and sadness, and pride and humility. I experienced a perfectly surreal moment when you laugh and cry at the same time. The moment that most of us only read about or see in movies. Even though I was fighting back tears, I couldn't help but feel blessed. I could smile at all the doubters, and I could cry and laugh with joy because I beat the odds. It seemed my life was summarized well in the following quote by Eleanor Roosevelt: "You gain strength, courage, and confidence by every experience in which you really stop to look fear in the face. You are able to say to yourself, 'I have lived through this horror. I can take the next thing that comes along...' You must do the things you think you can't do."

Obviously, the so-called experts didn't know or understand the passion, desire, and tenacity I prided myself on. They didn't know my struggles or that it was those very struggles that kept the fire in my heart raging. They didn't know that I played for more than wins, losses, and money in every game I played. Every game, I was playing to save myself. They had no idea that the basketball court gave me a place to deal with frustration, pain, and insecurities. Instead of letting those things rule my world, I used them as gasoline to power my engine and fuel my fire. Anyone who has ever watched me play knows that I played the game of basketball with my heart on my sleeve. I poured every ounce of myself into every single play. When my team lost, I viewed it as my failure alone, and I didn't feel right again until my team was back on the winning side.

As I sat at the Hall of Fame banquet listening to T. Boone Pickens being introduced, I realized that everyone has struggles, rich or poor. Everyone experiences hardship and loss, and good times and success. Yet, most people become overwhelmed by their circumstances and fall in the face of adversity rather than rise. The main difference between successful and unsuccessful people is the fact that successful people rise after a failure. They dust themselves off and get back in the game. Successful people use failure as a learning opportunity over and over again until they get it right. They never dwell on failure. That's what I try to do.

I have been poor and well off. I have had some fantastic highs as well as some miserable lows. At an early age, I learned that struggle is a part of everyone's life, and the only difference between my struggle and the struggle of others is how we choose to deal with it and react to it. As you read my story, you will see that statistically, I was doomed to fail. Still, hard work, the will and desire to overcome my circumstances, perseverance, and feeling comfortable in my own skin has helped me overcome any obstacle or hardship that crossed my path. It is crystal clear to me that every moment and detail of my life helped build my success story.

The crowd's ovation drew me out of deep thought as I heard my name being offered for induction. As I rose to take the stage, I was still trying to work out my speech in my head. I kind of knew what I was going to say, but I wanted to find the right words to articulate my feelings and preferably avoid crying. As I shook Governor Henry's hand and turned to the crowd, I could see the pride in my mom's eyes. In that instant, I knew there was no way I was going to be able to get through my speech without tears as childhood memories came flooding back.

1

Overcoming Obstacles

"The only thing that overcomes hard luck is hard work."

— *Harry Golden*

Growing up in a two-bedroom, one-bathroom home with rotting floors, two alcoholic parents, and four siblings, as well as rats and roaches, taught me how to persevere. Because of my parents' chronic alcoholism, I felt I had to take responsibility for my sisters and brothers. I grew up fast, out of necessity. But unlike many, our poverty didn't bother me. I didn't even realize we were poor until later in life when I could compare my experience with some of my friends' lives.

Now that I am older, I realize that growing up poor was both a constant struggle and a great blessing. As a child, I never realized how much I was learning about navigating life's ups and downs. Now, when I look back on my childhood experiences and stories, I am thankful for the lessons I learned. My past struggles were a form of teacher. I just never knew it.

The one thing in life that I am sure of is that God allows us to have certain life experiences, good and bad, to mold us into the best people we can be. Our stories are not written by chance. They are orchestrated, and every choice and decision we make, every obstacle we face and overcome, and every failure and success we experience is put in our paths to help us learn and be better people. Simply put, our lives are like a training camp that will either make or break us.

The humming of the box fan awakened me on this summer day. It seemed like the stickiness of humidity never went away. A fan, at least, moves the air and fools us into feeling cool for a moment. As I rubbed my eyes and turned over to look at my older brother, it dawned on me that I was about to be late. I jumped to my feet and hopscotched my nine-year-old self to the bathroom, carefully missing the rotting spots on the floor. Wiping the sleep from my eyes, I plopped some toothpaste on my finger and started brushing back and forth. Spitting it out and running to the closet, I dug through the clothes to find some jeans and a t-shirt. Hopping and pulling them on, I fell into the closet. The loud thump of my body on the floor woke my younger sister B.J.

"What are you doing?" she asked.

"I'm trying to get dressed, now go back to sleep."

"Where are you going?"

"I'm going to work. Do you want to come?"

"I'm too sleepy."

Out the door I ran, arriving at my cousin's house just in time. In full stride, he only lived about ten steps away. Just as I grabbed the screen door, Marvin exclaimed, "Dang! I didn't think you were going to show up!"

"Have I ever missed a day, man?!" I grabbed at his legs, trying to wrestle him to the floor.

"Stop girl! Quit playing," he snarled.

Marvin was my best friend in the whole wide world. We did everything together. You never saw one of us without seeing the other.

"Hey, you chillin' need to get out here," I heard Uncle Doc bark in his big burly voice.

"Come on man, before he leaves!" I grabbed Marvin's shirt and dragged him out of the door and into the back of Uncle Doc's truck.

Every day during the summer, we would wake up at 6:30 a.m., eat breakfast, and talk about all the things we were going to buy before school started. Then, we would hop in the back of Uncle Doc's truck and go up and down the side of the highways picking up aluminum cans. Sometimes we would go to busy highways, and other times, we would go to dirt roads. In our eyes, the results were the same—trash for cash. Every day was a different road to collect aluminum. It was hard work. It was hot, and it was dirty, but I had a reason to get up every day and do it. I liked having extra money in case my mom needed it to help buy groceries. Helping my mom always gave me a sense of pride, but I always secretly kept a little cash for myself. What I kept for myself was my secret.

Uncle Doc idled along while we walked the roadside using sticks that have nails in the ends to pick up the cans. Uncle Doc made the sticks so we didn't have to pick up the cans with our hands; hot pop and beer remnants were nasty—not to mention, there were always bugs inside the cans. We also avoided reaching into the grass and getting snake-bit. Uncle Doc was always concerned for our safety, but most importantly, he wanted to teach us the value of a dollar and that there is no substitute for hard work.

Some days we picked up cans for an hour, and some days we did it for longer. But it only felt like an hour as Marvin and I would get lost in our conversations about what we were going to do with our lives. At that age, we mostly only cared about getting some Nike shoes and a pair of Levi's jeans before school started, so we could have the same stuff the other kids had. As adults, we learn that the way someone dresses has little to do with how they are as a person, but when you're a kid, the clothes you wear at school and fitting in with your peers are everything.

That day's conversation was no different than any other day. Marvin yelled across the road, "You know I'm getting four pairs of jeans, three shirts, and a pair of Nikes for school this year!"

Since I never wanted him to top me, I shot back, "I'm getting the same except I'm getting two pairs of shoes this year!" That's what my mama promised.

He started laughing, "Girl you know you gonna have the same old corduroy pants with those blue patches on the knees, flooding as usual!"

I yelled back, "You don't know what I am going to get, an' you better shut up before I come over there and give you an Indian burn!"

"Just try it!" he challenged me. I loved Marvin, but sometimes he got under my skin. I threw down my bag and stick, ran across the road, and did a flying dive, similar to one I'd seen on the WWE, onto Marvin. We wrestled as though we were two grown men. No one would have thought that he was a fifth-grader and that I was a fourth-grader. Marvin was shorter than me and built like a lollipop. He had a big rounded head and thick bushy eyebrows; his body was small compared to his head. He looked like one of those bobblehead dolls. We always called him Baby Jesus because he never got in trouble. Meanwhile, I was tall and skinny with looping pig-tails. Everyone always told me I was going to be at least six foot three, but right then, I just looked like a stick person—the kind a kindergartener would draw.

Marvin got me down—then I rolled on top and had the upper hand. Next thing we knew, Uncle Doc snatched us both and yelled, "You two chillin' are always fighting! If I didn't know any better, I would think you hated each other. Now quit this nonsense before I do the whoopin'!" We both knew it was time to straighten up. Uncle Doc was not a little man by any means; he was a heavy man with very, very dark skin. He mostly played with us and told us jokes, but we had seen him angry enough to whip one of the kids twice. After that, neither of us wanted to be on the receiving end of one of Uncle Doc's whippings, so we both stopped struggling and tried to catch our breath.

I went back to my cans...

About an hour later, Uncle Doc yelled, "Come chillin', it's time to go eat something." We loaded up in the back of the truck and rode in silence back home.

My whole family lived in a cluster of shacks within a stone's throw of each other. We called it home. When we got there, I jumped out of the truck before it came to a complete stop and rushed into the house to wash my hands before Marvin. Everything was a competition, and I mean everything. We hurried and ate our sandwiches, then went outside and unloaded the cans. We put aluminum foil in the cans to make them heavier, smashed 'em, and then we were off to sell them. We stuffed the cans back into the bags and hopped in the back of the truck, eager to get to the nearest big town, Atoka. Our little town was called Stringtown. If you blinked while driving through it, you'd miss the whole town. Atoka, with three stop lights and a Walmart, was a big city to us.

We always stayed really close to Uncle Doc as he was weighing the cans. Neither of us wanted to get lost or left in the big city. Uncle Doc always got his pay, and then, he would pay us. Today, he got a little over forty dollars, so Marvin and I each received four dollars. We were in hog heaven. On the way back, I looked at Marvin and said, "We can start our own can picking business." His eyes got big, and he replied, "We can chop wood too. That should bring in the money. We can pick cans half the day and chop wood the other half. Let's shake on it."

As soon as we got to his house, I jumped out and yelled, "See you later." As I ran away, my worn tennis shoes kicked up the scorched Oklahoma red dirt behind me. I had to get to my secret hiding spot before anyone saw me. I ran to the side of my house, looked around to make sure no one was watching, pulled the tin house skirting away, and crawled under. I never had to worry about other people finding my money. The dogs were the only other animals to crawl under the house, and although Marvin knew I crawled under there, he was deathly afraid of the dark and wouldn't go under the house for all the Levi's and Nike shoes in the world. I took a dollar and put it in my jar, excited because I knew what I was going to spend it on. I quickly made my way back out from under the house before I could be spotted.

Picking up cans was a way for me to help my mother keep food in the house. I never let my pride get in the way, nor did I ever think I was too good to walk up and down the side of Highway 69 to pick up cans.

In today's world, too many people are embarrassed or think it's beneath them to do menial work. I was very proud of the fact that I was working to help my mom. Picking up those cans gave me a huge sense of pride. When we had nothing to eat, no single thing felt better than knowing I could crawl under the house and grab a couple of bucks to buy something to help my mother. Hard work never hurt anyone. I would much prefer being made fun of or disapproved of for picking up cans, than disgrace my name to get money.

2

Learning a Lesson in Baseball

"Baseball is like church. Many attend, few understand."

— *Leo Durocher*

One big summer event for me was none other than little league baseball. My cousin Stephan Brown was our coach, and he always let us ride to practice with him. It's probably illegal now to let kids ride in the bed of a pickup truck the way we did when we were kids. Even though I was a girl, I was the best pitcher in the five counties around my area and always the team's best player. Marvin was right on my heels. The only edge I had on him in baseball was that I wasn't scared of the ball. Marvin was so scared that Stephan had to put a bat behind his feet to keep him from stepping out of the batter's box when pitchers pitched him inside. Even though I was really good at baseball, the thing I loved the most about playing was the spitting. Of course, we couldn't dip Skoal, but boy, we'd eat sunflower seeds till the inside of our jaws got raw.

That year we were playing in the championship game. I'll never forget it. Stringtown, Oklahoma was a tiny town and proud of its little league team. I think you could tell how boring the town was just from the fact that the little league team was the talk of the town. We played Atoka, the big city I mentioned earlier where we'd sell cans with Uncle Doc. Atoka was about seven miles from Stringtown, but we didn't like any of the Atoka kids because they always thought they were better than us. This was our chance to finally shut them up. I was on the mound that day, rocking and firing. My infield was chanting it up, "Hey batter, batter, batter, batter. Swing, batter, swing." My heart was racing, but my mind was calm. It was a game right out of a movie.

All I had to do was strike out a couple batters, and then we'd have to score. As I got ready to deliver the first pitch, I heard, "Yea-hoo." My heart dropped. It was my dad. My dad never came to my games. Why was he here? "Yea-hoo" were words he only used when he was drunk. I felt like sticking my head in the nearest hole. Everyone already knew my father was the town drunk. Shoots, he should have been given a key to the jail as much as he went there for public intoxication. I released the first pitch. It was a wild pitch. I cursed in my head. Stephan immediately called time. By now, my mother was standing up and screaming at my father. They should have both been arrested for their behavior that day. Heck, it was a little league game, for pete's sake. Stephan walked out to the mound and took the ball out of my hands. He looked at me. Tears were welling up in my eyes. He said, "Are you okay?" I nodded my head yes while trying to push back the tears. I looked down at the ground. He put his hand under my chin and picked my head up. He looked me in the eyes and said, "Never put your head down because of your dad's actions. I know he is embarrassing you. You are a great kid. If you concentrate on striking out these two batters, no one will remember how your father acted. Come on, let's win this game." I looked up, said, "Okay," and finally regained control of my emotions.

He walked off the mound and back to the dugout; I threw the ball in my glove two times, kicked the dirt, spit, and put my foot on the rubber. I went into my stretch, checked the runner on first, mumbled to myself, "You can do it," and released the first pitch. "Strike," the ump bellowed, as my drunken father yelled out, "My daughter is better than all your punk boys!"

Two more pitches. Two more strikes. My mom finally ended up leaving the game, so my dad would leave too. Now I felt better, but Stephan's words lingered in my head. "Strike them out, and everyone forgets." The next batter came up, and I sat him down too. As I walked off the mound, Marvin came running up to me. He didn't dare hug me, but I knew that he knew I was truly bothered by what my dad had done. That's when Marvin stopped, seriously looked at me, and said, "You're the best." Now that I'm older, I know that that was Marvin's way of giving me comfort. He never openly admitted that I was better than him at anything. Hearing those words, though, coming from Marvin's mouth, made everything better.

We had the top of our order coming up. Mike Shields was hitting in the second hole, and he got a base hit. Marvin was up next, and he got a base hit too. I hit the four-hole. As the best hitter on the team, I always hit in the four-hole, and you could bet I'd almost always get on base. Today was no different. I got a base hit, so the bases were loaded. The next two batters struck out. We all put our rally hats on, then realized Randall McGee was up. Randall was one of the worst players on the team. We all thought it was over at this point. All we could do was pray for a miracle. Well, whoever believes that God doesn't answer prayers should have been at that game that day. Randall had a snowball's chance in hell of getting a hit. He fouled a couple off and took a couple of pitches. The count was 2-2 when the pitcher released a high rising fast ball. Randall jumped in the air, chop swung at that ball, and connected for a double. We scored two runs, and the game was over.

We jumped and celebrated as though we had won the World Series. Although we won the game and the bragging rights, Atoka ended up going to nationals in our place because we couldn't afford to go. I'll never forget what happened after that game; one Atoka kid came up to me and said, "Dang, you are good for a girl."

This was the day I realized that I was never going to let my parents' drinking problems, my life's struggles, other people, or my socioeconomic background determine who I would become in life. I decided I was never going to use those things as excuses. In fact, I was going to work as hard as I possibly could to be a success in everything that I did.

At some point in life, we all have to take ownership for our well-being. Life and free will are the two greatest gifts the Lord gave us. They're two of the only gifts you're given at birth that you don't have to work for. It's baffling to me why people give up on life and their dreams so easily. You're only given one life, so why wouldn't you fight to give yourself the best life possible?

On this day, my best friend Marvin and I pinky swore that our lives were going to be different. We promised we would push and pull each other to make sure we'd succeed. And we did just that. Marvin presently has two Master's degrees, a Ph.D., and has been with his wife for twenty years, and well, you're reading my story now. I think it's safe to say we kept our promise.

3

Racism Exists

*"If we were to wake up some morning and
find that everyone was the same race, creed
and color, we would find some other cause
for prejudice by noon."*

— *George Aiken*

Racism is something that I have a tough time with.
It's difficult for me to understand how, as humans in
the twenty-first century, a person can lack empathy
for another because of their skin color.

I believe sports is one of the very few places
where racism has no home and no place. Sports is
about being the best. To excel in sports, racism can
never exist because athletes care more about winning than anything else. Athletes know that winning is a team effort and for each player to work in
harmony, differences need to be put aside. Sports is

all about competition and being the best. Being the best has no color. Athletes want to compete against the best because it gives them the opportunity to achieve something great.

Basketball gave me the opportunity to travel the world, meet so many great people, and experience numerous other wonderful cultures. Those experiences opened up my heart and mind to things outside the realm of the southeastern Oklahoman mentality. I have Italian, Greek, Russian, Korean, Turkish, Polish, and Serbian friends, just to name a few. I am proud of the fact that each culture accepted me, mainly because I stepped outside my American box and tried my best to learn and live their cultures while in their countries. As Americans, we tend to expect others to speak English. I made it a point to learn as much of each country's language as I could. Looking back, I feel that they appreciated me for it.

It is baffling to me that I spent so much time in countries like Moldova, where I was the only black person I saw the whole time I was there. This is no exaggeration, yet I never experienced any racism. I have a hard time understanding why our country struggles so much with racism. I know history plays a part in it. But, how is it that people in other countries who don't look the same, don't speak the same language, and have a completely different belief system, can find a way to respect each other and each other's differences? Why is it so difficult for our country?

It's very unusual to experience racism in sports. I'm not saying that it doesn't exist, but it is rare. Athletes generally view and respect one another as competitors. It feels as though racism in sports is taboo and doesn't have a place among competitors.

I grew up playing six-on-six basketball. Most players don't even know what six-on-six means. Basically, players were not allowed to cross half court. There would be one team's guards and the other team's forwards on one side and vice versa in reverse on the other side. The guards would defend the other team's forwards, and once they either rebounded or took it out after the other team scored, the guards would dribble up to half court and throw it to their forwards. The forwards would in turn try and score on the other team's guards. Oklahoma was the last state to stop playing six-on-six in high school.

I'll never forget the night we played our biggest rival, a team from Byng, Oklahoma. They had one of the best programs in the state, and so did we, at Atoka High School. I always found it annoying that teams wanted to beat me. What I mean is, it always seemed as though teams were out to get me. I don't know why it seemed as though people took my talent personally. I wasn't a rude or disrespectful person, so it always hurt my feelings when I'd hear what other teams and coaches had to say about me. I understand a team wanting to win, but I'll never understand disrespectful or distasteful acts of players and fans; after all, it's just a game.

Most of my high school games were sellouts, so when Byng came to town, people would start lining up around four o'clock to make sure they got a seat before the fire marshal closed the door. I don't remember all the details of the game, but I do remember it was a close game and that they brought plenty of fans to support them. My mom always sat right behind our bench so she could yell at me. Her voice and my coach's voices were the only ones I seemed to be able to hear. My father was somewhere pacing around and probably angry because he felt as though I didn't warm up hard enough.

This game against Byng will always stand out in my mind because it was the only time I've ever experienced racism during a game. Throughout the game, the girl guarding me would drop the N-word. When she started with the name-calling, I knew right away her goal was to make me lose my temper so I would get ejected. That was probably the only way they could beat us. I told her, "I don't care what you call me, as long as you don't put your hands on me." It was getting late in the game, and I hadn't bitten into any of her tactics.

We were involved in a jump ball, and I suppose she decided to show me how tough she was. As she tried to rip the ball out of my hands, I let go, and down to the ground she went, on her knees. She popped up from the floor and came up to my chest. The only thing I'm thinking is, "Lord, please don't let me embarrass my family by dusting this girl off." I tried to keep my cool and had no intention of doing anything hostile until she completely crossed the line. In the end, she even had the audacity to spit in my face.

Now, please take into account the fact that she and I didn't know each other personally. I hadn't even said a word to her. I have yet to understand why she was so agitated or what I had done to provoke such low behavior from another human.

But one thing was for sure, I wasn't going to turn the other cheek on this. Before I even blinked, I smacked the taste out of her mouth. My mother taught us that spitting on someone was the worst thing you could ever do to a person. Spitting on someone warranted a true beat down in my house, and only my mom was doing the beating. All hell broke loose when I hit her.

My coach and I had both expressed to the referees that this girl was screaming racial slurs at me during the game, and they allowed it to go unchecked. So I don't totally feel at fault for what happened to her. Her father jumped up and started calling me names and headed to the court. Her father happened to be sitting near one of my cousins, so when he started calling me names and headed to the floor, my cousin Steve jumped in his path and got into a shoving match with him. The police later escorted them both out of the gym. My mother cleared the rails and also came to the court.

I was ejected from the game. I don't think she was ejected. Things went from good to bad fast. One of the referees vouched for me and kept me from having to sit the next game. I know that I never want to win anything so bad that I'm willing to use racial slurs or spit on someone to do it. I never experienced anything like this in sports before.

This high school experience affected me in the most profound way. As a player, you could seldom find me talking to another player during play. I allowed my playing to do the talking for me. I wasn't boastful or celebratory either. I always gave my opponent the utmost respect. I never wanted my actions to disrespect anyone. After being disrespected and humiliated during this game, I knew that was not the kind of attention I ever wanted to be a part of again.

My family didn't have a car until I turned sixteen. My mother and I usually walked a half-mile to the grocery store to get groceries. Our blue house sat on top of a hill, so coming home with a lot of heavy bags was a big chore.

I will never forget the time my mom and I were at the grocery store, and a man walked up to me and said, "Great game last night, Crystal!" I was a star basketball player by then; at least, that was what everyone else thought. On home game nights, the gym would always fill up to maximum capacity. The fire marshal typically had to shut the doors and started turning people away every time we played at home. If people wanted to watch us play, they had to arrive at the gym at least two hours early if they wanted to get in. People drove from all over to watch me play; the gym was always packed—not one empty seat, not even a place to stand in the whole building.

But this same guy that told me "Great game" always treated other black people like crap. "Nigger" was one of his favorite words to toss around when he saw black people. Because of this, when he approached me and tried to compliment me, I was livid. I looked around as if to say, I know you are not talking to me. By this point, I know he could see the look of disgust in my eyes, and he could definitely hear it in my voice when I said, "You can get your nigger-hating self out of my face. Just because I'm good at basketball doesn't mean I'm better than the other people you choose to call niggers."

You could feel the tension knife through all of us after I said those words. My mom stepped in between us and slapped me right in the face, and said, "He should have called you a nigger because you sure just acted like one." My mother's words and slap angered and confused me. "This man hates black people, Mama." I replied, still confused by what had just happened. She turned and grabbed my arm and said, "Crystal Robinson, two wrongs don't make a right. Do you hear me? Two wrongs never make a right. That was your chance to change his mind about black people. Instead, your reaction adds fuel to his flames. You had a chance to bridge a gap, and you missed it."

Inside, I immediately felt awful about the way I acted to this man. My mother was one hundred percent correct. I let an opportunity to impact someone's life for the better slip away from me. This incident weighed heavily on my mind for nearly a week. I saw this man several times after that incident, but I could never muster up the strength to walk up to him and apologize. This missed opportunity affected me in a positive way for the rest of my life. I learned that we are all different, we all have different beliefs, and all of our experiences program us to become the people we end up being. This experience left me with so many unanswered questions. Why is it so hard for us as a race to see past our differences? Why is it so hard for us to accept others for who they are? So many people confuse acceptance with condoning or supporting. I can completely accept the fact that someone chooses a different way of life than me, but it doesn't mean I have to agree with it. It also doesn't give me the right to hate, harm, or hinder this person. Hate only hurts the people who carry it in their heart. Physical pain is never infinite, but emotional pain will dwell and fester forever if you let it consume you.

4

Brokenness

"There are many ways of breaking a heart. Stories are full of hearts broken by love, but what really breaks a heart is taking away its dream—whatever that dream might be."

— *Pearl Buck*

My parents had a lot of knock-down-drag-out fights while I was growing up. I witnessed my mother break both of my dad's jaws as well as put a gun in his face.

Two alcoholics, no money, and three kids made for a bad situation no matter what day and age it was. My father was an ignorant drunk. He acted a fool most of the time. My mom often tried to calm him down, but that's when the fights erupted. My mom would hit my dad with stuff, anything she could get her hands on really, and my dad, to protect himself, usually ended up hitting her back.

One night during one of these drunken alterca-tions, my mom smashed my dad in the head with a hammer. All I recall is seeing blood gushing every-where; my dad was knocked out cold. My sisters, B.J. and Brandi, were screaming, "My daddy, my daddy!" I remember feeling bad, but I wasn't as distraught as my little sisters were. I had to remain calm for them. Plus, thinking about all the times that he had humil-iated me, I kind of thought he deserved to be hit, but definitely not killed.

My mother's nickname was Slim. After witnessing her drag this six-foot-six man outside, then return back in the house and start cleaning as if she had just taken the trash out, I knew I would never challenge her. I don't know if she thought he was dead or if she even cared. She never said a word to me about it. I began to get worried about him, so I went outside to check on him. Not knowing exactly what to do, I just laid beside him for a while.

As I lay there next to my dad, several things crossed my mind. How could two people who were supposed to love each other treat one another so poorly? And, if this is what love is, I hope and pray that I never fall in it, step in it, or encounter it. Since I had been taught that if someone experiences a con-cussion they shouldn't sleep, because if they did, they could slip into a coma, I started trying to wake my dad up.

My grandfather, who lived nearby, always tried to stay out of their messes, so I knew it was no use running to him. My mom had also always warned us that if we ever bumped our head, we should try to stay awake and not sleep because we might slip into a coma. She still didn't seem too concerned about my dad, though.

I knew that my dad had been hit very, very hard, and I could see that he was bleeding a lot; the wound on his head was really bad. I could tell that he needed stitches. His clothes and face had blood all over them. It was not a pretty sight. It seems that the alcohol in his system made him bleed profusely. I didn't know what else to do, so periodically, I would go out, shake him, and call his name until he responded in some sort of way. This was the only thing I knew to do to try and keep him from going into a coma. He lived, woke up with a hangover, and went to the hospital to get twelve stitches.

This hammer attack happened on a Sunday, which was no surprise. Mom and Dad always fought and cursed each other on the weekends because he either drank or gave away his whole paycheck over the weekend. When that happened, we all did without, unless I had enough money in my secret spot.

As children or adults, we are not always prepared for the different situations that arise in our lives. We can only make decisions to the best of our ability at the time and pray that we handled things correctly.

In my life, I had to figure things out as I went to overcome situations or challenges at hand. As long as we are breathing, obstacles are always lurking around the corner. The sooner we understand and embrace the fact that problems will always be a constant in life, the easier it becomes to deal with them. Most people spend too much energy focusing on problems instead of focusing on solutions. No one has an easy life. Challenges are not unique to you. They are universal. Despite what most people think, wealthy people have just as many, if not more, problems and stress than poor people. Money does make life easier at times, but it also comes with its own set of problems. Find a way to be thankful for whatever life throws your way, and stay positive.

I went through a period in my life where I felt lost in the dark. I was broken on the inside. It was especially difficult because I was a very young child with these major emotions. Emotions that I had no idea how to deal with. I didn't have the luxury of a strong family support system, nor did I feel as though I could talk to anyone. It was a terrifying time in my life, but God is good, and He is always on time. We just have to pay attention and recognize the gifts He sends us. That's the hard part though. Our gifts do not always come with a big yellow flag blowing in the wind. Sometimes our gifts come disguised as something else; sometimes, they are concealed as additional obstacles, but trusting in something bigger than your problems is where faith is born.

I constantly walked around as a child telling myself, "I know there is more to life than this." I did not know what it was, but I knew it existed somewhere.

At some point in each of our lives, we feel lost and broken. We simply have to pay close attention during these moments because as sure as my name is Crystal Robinson, God will send us the things we need to not only survive but to persevere. Sometimes we miss the answers because they are not always given to us exactly how we ask for them.

I have a friend who couldn't have kids. He prayed and prayed for his wife to get pregnant. He just wanted one child to carry on his lineage. The pressure he placed on himself and his wife caused her to pursue comfort somewhere else. He found out because she got pregnant. He had been praying for a child for so long with his wife. Now she was expecting another man's child. I feel as though he got exactly what he prayed for. The question then was, was he strong enough mentally to stay with his wife and raise the kid with her? The answer is yes. They have been married twenty some odd years and found a way through that struggle to build an even better relationship. Experience has taught me that we have to be strong enough to accept what has been given to us because things don't always come to us in the fashion we ask for them. I truly admired him for choosing to stick it out with her because some men's pride wouldn't allow them to stay.

Some of the lessons we are taught are dark lessons—like the night of one particular party. It was a night like many other nights when Mama had friends over listening to loud music, drinking, smoking, and having a good time. I must have been only ten years old. Usually, I stayed up all night during her parties because there was no sleeping with all the noise. Unlike my mother, it generally took me a couple of days to recover from her parties.

Our house had two bedrooms and one bathroom.

Everyone had to go through my sisters' bedroom to get to the bathroom. My mom had this one friend who was actually our cousin. He was an older man who most people liked. He and my dad shot dice together along with my cousin Loretta. But I hated him. He was nothing but a nasty old man to me. On the nights he came to Mama's parties, he would go to the bathroom and stop in my bedroom on the way and touch me all over. He would say, "You know how your mama borrows money from me when you ain't got no food? I won't give y'all nothing if you don't lay there and be quiet." He did things to me that I still wish I could forget, but at least he was doing it to me and not my sisters.

I loved my sisters and tried to protect them the best I could. In this case, that meant I had to let him have his way with me. These were my reasons for not saying anything. My parents never suspected a thing; they were living high, having fun, and getting drunk. I would never tell a soul if that meant my sisters might get hurt or go without food more than we already did.

I had an older brother, but he was an alcoholic by the seventh grade and usually was nowhere to be found, even if I wanted to ask for help. In moments like this, I decided that if my parents weren't going to protect us, then it was my duty to protect my little sisters by any means necessary.

I was in the third and fourth grade at that time. Even at such a young age, I was disgusted with myself. When my mother had those parties, I knew it was my night to feel like the dirtiest person in the world. It was as though I was in a bad dream that I just couldn't wake up from. As horrible as this made me feel, it was also the time that I learned to sacrifice myself for those I love truly. To this day, I feel that sacrifice is one of my biggest strengths and one of my biggest weaknesses. At the time, I just kept telling myself, "You are protecting your sisters. You have to do this." That's exactly what got me through it. I had always loved my family more than I loved myself, so if anyone was going to do without or suffer, I figured it might as well be me.

Although this was one of the most trying times in my life, I genuinely believe I was and still am emotionally stronger than both of my sisters. This was my burden to bear because I knew it would have affected them differently. This wasn't easy for me to deal with at the time, but I wouldn't go back and change it if it meant that either of my sisters would have to suffer in my place.

There is no quote truer than Friedrich Nietzsche's, "That which does not kill us makes us stronger." I have never sat around feeling sorry for myself, asking God why he let this happen to me. It was a horrible part of my life that I chose to let shape me for the better. If I elected to allow these dark days to ruin my life, I would have been putting limits on my life and my ability to overcome hardship. As a child, when I was unable to protect myself, that friend of Mama's had already made me feel like the lowest piece of scum; I refused to let that carry over and ruin anything else in my life. I decided right then and there that I would never be anyone's victim.

5

The Death of a Friend

*"Death is more universal than life; everyone
dies but not everyone lives."*

— *Alan Sachs*

One day while in class at Southeastern Oklahoma
State University, a girl named Sabrina Crain tapped
me on the shoulder and handed me a note. I knew
her from high school. She was younger than me, but
everyone knew everyone, since we went to a small
high school. We were never really friends, but her
brother Chris and I graduated together, so I was anxious to see what the note said.

I opened the note, and it said, "Did you hear about
Chris?"

I wrote back, "No, what did he do this time?"

During a specific period in my life when I just
wanted to die, Chris was one of my running buddies.

34

I stayed at his house a lot and we would often sneak out his window and drive to Dallas. We played Russian roulette. We played chicken with the trains. One of us would sometimes stand on the cab of his truck while the other drove around trying to throw the other one off the truck. These were just a few of the dangerous games we played. He and I were usually drinking heavily when we were together. I was running from being gay, and he was trying to get his parents' attention. He constantly said his parents didn't care about him, and he wished he could die, but I was always reassuring him that they cared about him, and he was just being a brat.

Chris was one of my best friends. Even though he didn't have an athletic bone in his body, he was the one who cheered and yelled the loudest at my games. He was a good dude. In high school, when my mother wouldn't allow me to do something, I would say to her, "If you let me do this, I'll buy you a twelve pack of beer." Sometimes she agreed, and Chris would always willingly give me the money to buy her the beer. Very few people knew how close Chris and I were.

Chris and I could really relate to one another, maybe because we both carried an empty feeling around with us. I truly think this is what drew us to one another. I often snuck in his window late at night. On nights that we were sneaking off and driving to Dallas to hang out, we'd spend countless hours talking about our families. His dad was a doctor, and he lived in one of the biggest homes in our town. He even received a brand-new truck when he turned sixteen. Our lives were on complete ends of the spectrum, yet we both had misery in our hearts and minds, and therefore found peace with one another. He loved bringing me lunches in high school.

Sabrina tapped me on the shoulder and handed me the note back. I opened it up, but wasn't prepared for what it would say; it read, "He died last night. He got hit by a train." I couldn't believe what I was reading; it felt as though the walls were closing in on me. Suddenly, I couldn't breathe. I found myself fighting back tears. I was about to choke on them.

I started gathering my things as quickly as I could. I was making so much noise, knocking my books and everything else off the desk. I knew the whole class was staring at me. The professor finally asked, "Crystal is everything okay?"

"Yeah, yeah," I responded while still trying to process what I had just read, "I need to leave."

I was very visibly upset and disturbed. I ran out of the classroom and leaned against the wall to catch my breath. I couldn't fight the tears back any longer; they started streaming down my face. I tried to avoid everyone on my way back to my dorm room. As soon as I got into my room, I threw my books against the wall and slumped to the floor. My suitemate knocked on the door and asked if everything was okay.

"Go away, Mary," I yelled. She left me alone. All I could think about was the fun, stupid things Chris and I had done together. I had not seen him in a long time. He had moved back to New Mexico with his mother after his parents got divorced. I kept thinking, "If only I had been there for him." It was really difficult for me to come to terms with his death. I had experienced death many times before, but for some reason, this was different. This one was really hard for me. I couldn't help but think that I should have told someone about his state of mind and how he felt. We had so many discussions about our lives. I just never thought it would come to this.

For the next few days, I was in a stupor. Dr. Parham, the athletic director, called me into his office and asked me what happened and why I left class. I told him I found out by note that one of my friends had died. He said, "That's not the way to tell someone that her friend died." He asked if I was okay, and I told him I didn't really want to talk about it anymore. He got the hint and quickly dismissed me.

As I was dressing for the funeral, I stopped for a minute and sat on the couch. Thoughts of Chris kept running through my head. I could see his smile, and I started to cry. I stood up but sat right back down. I couldn't bring myself to go to his funeral. I tried to find the strength, but it was not in me. I sat there dressed for his funeral but did not go. I regret that to this day. I felt such a horrible sense of guilt, and I could not shake it. In a way, I felt as though it was my fault. I spent many nights with Chris, listening to him cry and complain. He had so much pain in his heart, and I never told anyone. I thought I was just being a good friend, but maybe I should have told someone. Today, I'm sure I should have.

Death has this way of leaving an unshakable pain that seems to linger in our hearts forever. We each develop our own way to deal with the pain that loiters in our hearts and minds, but somehow, someway, we have to try to find the good in the things that have hurt us the most.

My friend Chris was a great example of what brokenness can do to a person. He was broken, like me, but for different reasons. He felt like his parents did not love him, even though I know they loved him very much. This taught me how important perspective can be.

Allowing yourself to continue to be broken inside from negative events will always prove to be detrimental to your state of mind. Allowing pain to fester in our hearts without help or guidance leads to widespread infection, poisoning us with pain and suffering. There is so much strength to be gained in asking for help. Don't hide the pain in your heart because that pain can best be carried by allowing others to carry it with you. Carrying it alone is too heavy a burden.

6

Lost and Confused MVP

*"Accepting yourself doesn't mean you can't
change anything about yourself, it means
recognizing who and what you are, and then
making the most of it."*

— *Jappreet Sethi*

By the time I was a senior in high school, I was
recruited by every college team in the country! It
was hard to believe that a game I grew up playing
with my cousins was about to pay my way through
college! I had no idea where I wanted to go. I just
knew I wanted to experience something other than
Oklahoma. Louisiana Tech was one of the NCAA
powerhouses then. I had lots of family in Monroe,
Louisiana and it was only seventy miles from the
university. I remember having such a good experience when I moved in with my grandmother for a

year in high school that it just felt like a good fit.

My college coach really encouraged me to make visits to other schools, but I had pretty much made up my mind that I was attending Louisiana Tech. The only thing that bothered me about going there was the fact that they wanted me to quit playing baseball on the boys' high school team. I started at second base in my sophomore and junior years. I spent most of my freshman year pinch hitting for our catcher. I'd been playing baseball with these guys since the first grade. It kind of broke my heart when I quit!

I had no idea what to expect when I set foot on the campus. I was so excited to get there until I realized exactly what it was going to take to be a high-level college athlete. Neither my heart nor my body was ready for the workload. We spent time on the track field and in the weight room. These were two things I'd never really done before because I really didn't like them. My high school coach also coached track, and he had a rule that if you played basketball, you had to run track. I ran my first year and finished third in the state in long jump and the 200-meter dash. The two girls who beat me in both events were seniors. I didn't particularly like running track because it was freezing when you arrived at the meet, and by the time you left, you were three to four shades darker because of the sun. After track was over in my freshman year, I told my coach that I would transfer to another school if I had to be a track star too. I think he stopped coaching track so that he wouldn't have to change his rules.

The workload, plus the fact that I felt like I didn't relate to anyone on my team except for Vickie

Johnson, made me uncomfortable. What made it worse was when some of my teammates invited me to go to Grambling University to hang out at a party. I sat in a corner by myself most of the evening, and then they left me at the party. Looking back, I was a big baby, but at the time I was scared. I was a rural kid who had never spent much time around inner-city kids. It was a bit of a culture shock for me, believe it or not!

I got really depressed and started seeing a counselor at Louisiana Tech. I found myself in a place where my past struggles seemed to be catching up to me. It was crushing me. I was always on the verge of tears. I spent time with the counselor twice a week, but no one knew about it. During the talks with my counselor, we figured out that I had some deep-seated issues that were not going to go away. We talked about all the things that I had been through in my life, and we talked about basketball.

I told my counselor about wanting to die. I poured everything out to her. It was really easy talking with her. She listened intently, asked a few questions, and never judged me. She told me that I had to find a place that made me happy. She said that the amount of stress I was putting on myself was way too much for someone my age. She suggested that I should be near or with my family, but I loathed my parents. They were the last people I wanted to be around. I was very angry with them. I felt as though they had not protected me as a child. I hated the fact that they drank like fish. I hated the fact that my father was like Otis on *The Andy Griffith Show* for most of my life. I hated the way they would fight with each other.

I have never seen two people more disrespectful to each other than them.

I needed to leave Louisiana Tech, but I didn't have any idea where to go. The last time I felt this hopeless was when I was a child, and my parents, my siblings, and I were in my mom's little Chevette. My father was driving, and he was drunk. They started fighting. My father threatened to pull out in front of a big truck and kill us all. I remember crying and begging, "Please don't kill us." My mother was slapping and hitting my dad yelling, "You better let me and these kids out of this car." Finally, she got the door unlocked and we hurried out. My dad peeled off. At that moment, I felt so helpless, and I had no idea what to do to get out of this situation.

Looking back, I wish my parents had coerced me to stick it out. My mother never allowed us to start a project and quit, so I was very shocked when she told me it was okay to come home if I was having problems. Leaving Louisiana Tech was one of the toughest decisions I've ever had to make. It feels awful to let people down, but I decided to go back home, regroup, and decide where I would go to school next. I still think about how things would have turned out had I stayed at Louisiana Tech, but I feel I learned a lot about myself from this major decision.

By the time I got back home, every university in the U.S. was calling and trying to get me to transfer to their school. Honestly, I had no idea which school I would select. I thought about Tennessee. Pat Summitt was and arguably still is the greatest coach of all time. The University of Oklahoma was in the back of my mind, because it was the state university that tried the hardest to recruit me. Once I got home to Oklahoma, I realized that not much had changed. My hometown reminds me of a soap opera; you can miss the entire show for three years and start watching it again, and nothing has changed.

After much thought and deliberation, I decided to take my talents to Southeastern Oklahoma State, an NAIA school thirty miles from my hometown. This was a very unpopular decision, but I've never been one who liked following the crowd. I had the opportunity to select any Division I school in the country, but I chose an NAIA school that was 1-26 in regular season play.

My critics thought I went there because I was afraid of competition. I selected Southeastern Oklahoma State because I wanted to put the area where I grew up on the map! It takes a lot to change a program and still find ways to play at a high level, especially when defensive strategies are keying in on stopping you. It was no easy feat! My leadership skills and my game had to evolve! I learned so much about myself during this period, and as an added bonus, my friends and family were able to witness every aspect of my college career. Going to a big school was the popular thing to do. It's what all players of my caliber did. I feel that this decision marked the first step in taking control of my life and making it what I wanted it to be.

I played the second semester and we won a few more games, but it wasn't enough to impact the season. My freshman year came and went without notice. During my sophomore year, we made a lot of noise. I was number one in the country in scoring.

I received Player of the Week several times, and the fire marshal had to close the gate every game. The crowds were amazing; even the hallways were packed. The way our team impacted Southeastern was insane! People were driving from Kansas, Arkansas, and Texas to watch us play. We made it to the NAIA National Tournament but didn't get very far. At the end of the season, my college coach actually told me that I was too unselfish, and if we wanted to really go far in the playoffs, I would have to do more. I averaged thirty points a game and had numerous fifty-point performances; I really didn't know what more he thought I could do! I suggested to him that we needed a few more players who could help. My assistant coach, Brett Frank, went out and found those players. I decided to focus my energies on my leadership skills; the next season would be the best by far. I was having so much fun. I no longer spent too much time focusing on the things that had caused me to get sidetracked before. I felt a lot of happiness and joy at my new home!

My junior year in college was the first time I was named the NAIA Tournament MVP. My team lost in the finals, but I still received the MVP honor. It is seldom that a player on the losing team receives this honor. While I appreciated the recognition, I couldn't find any joy in my heart for winning that award. As a matter of fact, I took the trophy and gave it to the other team's best player. "This kind of award doesn't matter if you don't win," I kept telling myself.

I literally felt as though I was in physical agony from losing that game. It felt like I had let my team and coaches down. It was at this moment that I realized that losing was not an option for me. "I never want to feel this feeling again," I kept telling myself. I began to throw myself into the game even more than I already had. I watched every game I could, and I played every time I could. I asked questions and constantly talked basketball with anyone I could learn from. Quite frankly, I decided to become a student of the game, and all of my hard work paid huge dividends. My skills and knowledge became so astute that I felt as though I was in control of every game, whether we were losing or winning.

I learned how to impose my will on the game, and I figured out the secret to being great. It was quite simple in fact: earn the respect of your teammates and give them their time to shine, so when the game is on the line, they don't care how much you have to shoot. Just like I cared about my sisters more than myself, I also cared about my teammates more than I cared about myself or any awards. I could have averaged fifty points per game and shattered national records had I been a selfish person, but I learned that putting my teammates and winning first felt way better than any trophy. I scored what I had to score to win games, whether it was ten points or sixty points, and my teammates respected me for that. My belief in them gave them the courage and confidence to make shots when the games were close. We won a lot of basketball games following my formula, and through that, everyone was happy and on the same page. I led with humility, and they followed with honor.

My senior year was almost identical to my junior year. I was an NAIA All-American, an NAIA National

Tournament MVP, and set and broke record after record at Southeastern Oklahoma State University. But in the end, I felt as though I was just a loser, a runner-up with a ton of accolades. At least, that's how I viewed it. Somewhere, somehow during my college years, I became an extreme perfectionist. I never gave attention to the things I did well. I spent most of my time dwelling on the things I did poorly. Perhaps my dad helped to train me to think this way.

As a third-grader, I remember coming home excited about scoring thirty points in a fifth- and sixth-grade game. Rather than celebrate with me or praise me for my play, my dad would say, "What about the four shots you missed? And, what about those two turnovers?" He never told me that I had done a good job or patted me on the back; he always said, "You could have done better." In fact, he did this after every game. My dad wasn't a very affectionate person, he didn't have many friends and often had trouble relating to others. I can count on one hand the number of times that I remember my dad telling me he loved me or that he was proud of me. I know he cared about me and my success because he couldn't even sit down at my games, he was more nervous than I was. I was an adult when I finally understood that he loved me very much. It was his way of challenging me to perform better. My dad was a six-foot-six scoring guard who often dominated Robert Parish. Maybe he felt as though his life fell short of what it was destined to be. I believe that's why he never allowed me to get too comfortable with my performance on the court.

What I know is: it's a horrible feeling to

overcome and accomplish so much and still feel like an unworthy loser inside. This seemed to be the burden I had to bear for the remainder of my life. The only time I didn't notice this feeling was when I was with my best friend Marvin. He and I were truly kindred spirits. Whenever that unworthy feeling would surface inside of me, I would think about the times we spent talking about the funny things we did as children. I believe the many stories we created comforted me because he knew everything about me. He knew what my childhood was like. He knew where I came from. He knew who I was and what I was, and he loved me wholeheartedly despite it all.

By this time, my talents were creating quite the buzz around Oklahoma and other states. Southeastern Oklahoma State University witnessed and enjoyed some of the most exciting women's basketball in the school's sports history during my time there. Our games were a guaranteed sell out. On basketball game nights, people had to be in line at least two hours before the game started to get a seat. It was like my high school games all over again. People were driving from other states to see me play. It seemed as though everyone wanted a little piece of me. This feeling made me very uncomfortable; I have never handled popularity easily. To this day, I'm still embarrassed when someone asks for my autograph. I just couldn't understand why anyone would want my signature. I viewed myself as a loser. I felt as though I was just someone who always got close but never quite got there. I never viewed myself as autograph worthy. I mentally created a negative image of myself; I thought that if people knew what my life was really like they would never want my auto-graph. I felt as though this shame followed me like a shadow. I experienced some sunny days, but the shadow was never too far behind, always looming and always lurking.

I couldn't bring myself to tell anyone about these negative feelings. I tried very hard to keep everyone at a distance. I didn't want fans because that would have brought about too much conversation. At times, I had this overwhelming urge to blurt out my life story to strangers. Careful not to let that happen, I avoided as many conversations as possible with others. Even the people who knew me well have never had a clue about the feelings and thoughts I had corrupting my head and hardening my heart.

On the outside, I was on top of the world, but I was lost and confused on the inside. It seemed as though my soul was wandering or searching for something. I never found happiness in accolades or accomplishments. In fact, more than half of the trophies I've ever received, I've given away. Yet, so many athletes today let accomplishments and acco-lades define who they are as people. Basketball has given me many wonderful memories, and has taken me around the world and back, but it's never defined me. For some reason, the game of basketball has never been able to fill the empty void I carried inside of me. Throughout college, I kept telling myself, "There has to be more to life than this."

7

Accepting Myself

"Acceptance is not submission; it is acknowledgment of the facts of a situation. Then deciding what you're going to do about it."

— *Kathleen Casey Theisen*

Accepting ourselves and others has always been and always will be a daunting task for us as human beings. As a society, we emphasize wearing trendy clothes, fitting in with the cool crowd, and being liked by everyone. In reality, these things don't even really matter in such a short, fleeting life. In the grand scheme of things, life is finite. The only things that we should be defined for are our actions and how we treat others. I spent many dejected years of my life trying to measure up to society's standards so others would accept me.

In the third grade, it became obvious that I was completely different from the other girls. Not only was I the best athlete in town, boy or girl, but I hated Barbie dolls and most "girly" things. In my opinion, Barbie dolls were made for blowing up with fire-crackers. I'd rather dig up worms and play with snails than brush hair and wear dresses. I wasn't the only one to notice my difference either; my mom started making me wear dresses, hoping to force me into being a girl.

One time, my mom made me sit on the porch in a dress and watch all of my male cousins play football. That was torture for me. I belonged out there. I was better at football than any of them ever thought about being. How could she do this to me? So I devised a plan. Every time she made me wear a dress, I would go out and play so hard that I came back with it ripped, torn, and dirty as hell. I was willing to take a whoopin' for that any day. In the end, I won. I wore her down. She stopped making me wear dresses—I guess she got tired of whoopin' me.

It was in third grade that I realized I didn't like the same things other girls liked. This was also when I realized that I liked them. This feeling left me with a ton of questions. Am I the only girl who feels this way? Why do I feel this way? I wished I had someone to talk to, but there was no way I was going to tell anyone.

Third grade was also the year that I started my relationship with God. It was a trying, difficult time, to say the least. Here I was in the third grade with all of these unexplained emotions. I had no idea what that kind of love was or meant. Heck, my parents never seemed to really like each other, let alone love each other. I had a million questions, but no one to ask them to.

This was the same year I started playing organized basketball. Basketball was my enjoyment; I played it all the time. When we were home and had the chance, my cousins and I would play from dusk until dawn. Both of my parents were NJCAA All-Americans, so I guess you could say it was instilled in me early on.

Looking back on my life, it's almost shocking to realize how everything that ever happened to me was tied to basketball. As a third-grader, I was a starter on the fifth- and sixth-grade team. People would come from all around to see the third-grader play. It is not normal to see a third-grader score thirty points. But heck, I was scoring forty points a game.

It was thanks to basketball that I met Brother Les Peevyhouse. He was the preacher at First Baptist Church, which all the white people in Stringtown attended. My family stopped going to church a while ago as the black church was no longer active.

One day, Brother Les attended one of our games and saw me play. After the game, he came by me and told me what a great player I was. He invited me to church and gave me a piece of candy. After that day, he never missed a game and would always tell me how well I had played. It became a routine. One day he showed up on my side of town in the church van. My cousins and I were running around playing outside when he pulled up. As soon as I recognized who it was, I ran out to greet him.

"Hey, Brother Les," I blurted out.

"Hello Crystal," he replied while giving me a hug. "Is your mother or father home?" he asked.

"My mom is in the house," I stated.

He kind of patted me on the head, the way a person would do to a cute little puppy, as he walked past me and headed to the door. As my mom answered the door, I couldn't help but feel embarrassed when they disappeared into our ragged house. We were very poor and didn't have much, but what we did have, my mom was psycho about keeping clean. In fact, she was a huge clean freak; that didn't make much sense to me at the time because we lived with rats and roaches. It wasn't long before Brother Les came strolling out with this big smile on his face. "Your mother said you can come to church if you would like," he stated.

I felt a little wave of panic come over me after he said that. I had been putting Brother Les off for a few months now. He had asked me to come to church after every game, and now he was on the black side of town, coming to my house, and asking my mom if I could go to his church. That's the moment I realized that I couldn't run from Brother Les anymore. I figured out that it was just better to go and get it over with, so he would leave me alone.

"I will come Sunday if I can get a ride," I responded. My family didn't have a car, and even though I walked all over the place, my mom would have never let me walk to the other side of the tracks at night. Surely that would give me a good enough excuse to not go to church.

As this thought was crossing my mind, Brother

Les said, "Don't worry. I will pick you up in the church van and bring you home after church."

"Okay," I answered, feeling sick inside about committing myself to go.

I didn't really know how to deal with the way church made me feel inside. I had a myriad of emotions that ranged from shame and hurt to comfort and confusion. The preacher just told me I could tell God anything, and he would love me despite what I told him. "Does this kind of companionship and love really exist?" I asked myself. I didn't really know the answer to that question, but if it did exist, it was exactly what I needed right then. After hearing what he said though, I knew church would definitely be in my future.

I started catching the church van to church every time it opened. I went to Sunday school, Wednesday night church, and vacation Bible school. I talked all of my friends into coming to church too. It went from just me and Brother Les in the church van to the van being full. Even the kids who rode to church with their parents, now wanted to ride the church bus with us.

God and I became close friends during that time. I shared all of my secrets with Him, and in return, He spoke to my heart. Through that, I began to see things differently. I finally saw an escape from all of my pain and sorrows.

I started to feel compassion for other people that I had never felt before. I learned to compromise and see strengths in people instead of weaknesses. I began picking the nerdiest, most unathletic kids to be on my basketball team first. Before I started going to church, I couldn't care less if they got to play or not; I was content watching them sit on the ground beside the court while they watched the real athletes play. But now, I cared. I knew my team would win either way; I felt good letting them be a part of that. In return for picking them first, they helped me with my math, taught me how to play chess, and educated me on how to make word searches. I now realize that I mastered the art of give-and-take at an early age.

Church seemed to be a mixture of good and bad things for me. It gave me all of these peaceful and kind feelings and thoughts, but at the same time, I felt an unbelievable amount of shame and guilt because I knew I was nothing like the girls around me. I never asked for these feelings. I wanted to be like all of the other girls. At this stage in my life, I was so young that I didn't really let the way I felt inside bother me too much. I ignored it and poured myself into basketball; it was just so much easier to live in the light of my talent.

Basketball was the one place where I could forget all of the darkness I was feeling inside. I was invincible on the court. No one could hurt me, and I knew God would keep my secret.

8

The Struggle Inside

"Any fool can know. The point is to understand."

— Unknown

The older I got and the clearer my sexuality became, the more I wanted to die. I struggled all through high school with my identity. On the outside, I was happy, and everyone loved me. No one knew my struggles except me. Growing up in a small town in the middle of the Bible Belt was an every-day challenge for someone like me. Everyone would hate me if they knew that I was attracted to girls. I wanted to be like everyone else, but the thought of being with a guy made me want to throw up. Not a day went by that I didn't pray that I would die. I wanted this day to be the last day for me rather than pretend to be someone I am not.

"Lord please allow me to come home today. Please don't let me spend another day like this. I can't fight this monster inside of me." This was my prayer.

There were many nights where I sat with a gun in my mouth, sobbing hysterically. I wanted to pull the trigger so badly, but the fear of going to hell for taking my own life kept me from doing it. I felt alone. I never slept. I just couldn't seem to turn my mind off.

In my freshman year of high school, my family moved to Atoka for me to play basketball. My father played college basketball with Coach Daniel, the coach at Atoka High School. I was angry about this move for two reasons. First, I grew up disliking the Atoka kids. They always thought they were better than us because we were from such a small town. Secondly, they were called the Atoka Wampus Cats. I didn't want to be called a Wampus Cat. What was a Wampus Cat anyway?

It felt very uncomfortable trying to make friends in Atoka. A few of the girls on the basketball team liked me, while others hated me. I think they hated me because they felt threatened by my abilities as a basketball player. The ones that didn't like me never tried to get to know me, so there was no way I was going to try to get to know them. Firstly, we had nothing in common besides basketball and secondly, I was frightened that I might start to like one of them. So, I made sure to keep my distance.

I ended up hanging with one of my cousins and

his friends. They were a pretty wild bunch of seniors who partied often. They taught me a lot that year. You know, it was stuff we never learned in textbooks. I learned about chasing whiskey with beer, speed shifting, deer hunting, and reckless driving.

My cousins and his friends were exactly what the doctor ordered. I found my way to die without doing it to myself. It was as though I had found my loophole in the rules. Most of the things we engaged in were things where someone could have easily gotten hurt or killed. I was game for anything they wanted to do. Bring on the good times.

While Coach Daniel was teaching me different aspects of basketball, my friends were teaching me how to really live life. Coach Daniel was teaching me about reading the defense and shot selection; my friends were teaching me how to surf on top of moving cars, play chicken, and play Russian roulette.

Outside of basketball, car surfing was one of my favorite things to do. We did it two different ways. The most dangerous way was my favorite because the amount of pain one could feel was incredible. I craved the pain. It reminded me that I was alive even though I felt dead inside. My friends and I would stand up in the back of the pickup truck while another friend drove. We had to keep standing while the driver sped and swerved, constantly trying to throw us off our feet. We'd be thrown all over the bed of that truck, we'd smash into the cab of the truck and into each other, and then when we finished, we had bruises everywhere. This was our idea of a good time. The more we surfed, the trickier we made it. We started standing up on the cab of the truck. The driver didn't try to throw us off, but he drove as fast as we could with us standing up there in the surfing position.

My friends and I became adrenaline junkies. The rush and surge of energy we felt after one of those rides was unmatched, but the more we did it, the more we began searching for a greater rush. Eventually, we graduated to more dangerous things. We played chicken with trains and even tried Russian roulette a couple of times. We drank a lot of Jim Beam and Jack Daniel's, and we chased it with beer.

One night at a party, I wasn't even there fifteen minutes, and I was lying in a ditch so drunk that I couldn't walk. We would make these big circles and pass the bottles of alcohol around. One person chugged while the others counted. After you downed a drink, you had to kill a bottle of beer. We were trying to see who could chug the longest. On this particular night, I was so drunk I ended up in my friend's bathtub vomiting everywhere.

My friends decided to take me home and leave me on the porch after knocking on my door. Not only was I sick for three days, but my mother tortured me by yelling in my face, slamming doors, and slapping me. That was the end of drinking for me. I had never been so sick in my life. I told God that I wouldn't drink again until I was responsible enough to know what I was doing. Even now, alcohol reminds me of that bad taste that you get after vomiting it. I was starting to lose my focus in life, and just like that, God put me back on the right path.

9

A Big Jump

*"There is no such thing as a 'self-made' man.
We are made up of thousands of others.
Everyone who has ever done a kind deed for
us, or spoken one word of encouragement
to us, has entered into the makeup of our
character and of our thoughts, as well as
our success."*

— *George Matthew Adams*

As a joke, I'd jump over people's heads. I'd run up behind them, jump in the air, and put my hands on their shoulders to get a boost up and over. One day at school, I jumped over this girl's head. That girl was Marci Cochran. Marci went home and told her dad, and he didn't believe her, so a few days later, she walked up to me and asked me to come home with her. I looked at her like she was crazy. Marci Cochran was one of the popular girls at school. Her family was wealthy, and even though I had jumped over her head, I didn't know her from Adam. "My dad doesn't think there is any way you can jump over my head," she said. "Can you come show him? I'll take you home afterwards," she explained. I was unsure about it all, but I agreed. Marci had a really outgoing personality, so it wasn't too surprising that she asked a ton of questions on our way over to her house. I don't really recall the particular questions, but I remember that she talked a lot.

We arrived at her house, and it was unlike anything I had ever seen. I only saw these kinds of houses on TV. I had no idea that I was about to meet the people who would play a major part in shaping and molding me as a person. We entered the house, and Marci started yelling, "Dad, Dad, Crystal is here." We waited a few minutes, and her dad emerged from the back of this huge house.

"Hey, Crystal. I'm Morris," he said as he hugged me, "Marci tells me you can jump over me."

I proudly responded, "Yes sir, I can."

"I have to see this to believe it," he responded.

We went outside, and I made him stand in a spot, and I backed up behind him and took off running. My heart was beating fast. I jumped off of two feet, put both hands on his shoulders, and flew right over his head. The landing wasn't great, but I made it. "Whoa, that's amazing, kid! Do it again," he said. So, I leaped over his head a second time, and from that day on, I was a part of the Cochran family. I soon began spending all of my free time at the Cochrans' house.

Morris and his wife Cindy had four kids: Marci, Mark, Mindy, and Mike. One day, I was sitting with

Cindy, and we were talking. Not talking about any-thing in particular, we were just talking. Cindy has this way of making you feel comfortable to talk to her about anything. Like Marci, she also asked a lot of questions, but for some reason, I wanted to share with Cindy. During this talk, she looked at me, hugged me, and said, "Morris and I are so thankful you came into our lives. You and your personality remind us so much of Mark. We feel like God sent you to us." I responded by saying, "I know God sent you guys to me." I can honestly say that this family was one of the most Christian, caring, loving, remarkable, sin-cere groups of people that I had ever met. I know I'm a better person because they came into my life; they set examples for me as well as for the whole community.

Morris walked in the door and said, "Hey, Crystal, wanna play some tennis?" This caught me by sur-prise since Morris and I usually played basketball.

"I don't know how," I answered.

"Oh, don't worry, you will learn fast. You're a great athlete," he responded.

"Let's do it," I said as I jumped up and ran to pick out my racket.

It was rough at first. Morris had to teach me the basic fundamentals of tennis, and he was correct: I picked it up in no time. He beat me the first couple of times, but I thrashed him regularly as I got older. After we finished hitting balls that first day, Morris said, "I remember the first time I saw you. I was the coach of a little league baseball team for Atoka. You were the pitcher, and you guys came from behind to beat us. None of us knew you were a girl until you took your hat off." We both started laughing. He said, "I'll never forget Mark saying, 'That's the best girl I've ever seen before in my life.'"

Mark passed away when we were in the eighth grade. He and a friend had just returned home from deer hunting, and the friend was messing around with his rifle. No one knows exactly what happened, but somehow, the gun went off. He accidentally shot Mark in the head at point blank range.

Mark and I had mutual friends, but I didn't know him that well outside of competing against him in various sports. I do know that he was really lively and always friendly to all of the kids I knew. Color didn't matter to him. He was an athlete, and I've found that most athletes don't see color. They might see skill and competition but never color. There's a sort of brotherhood among athletes. Everyone is striving to be the best in their respective sport. That's what allows athletes to relate to one another. Although I didn't know Mark well, my heart bled for his family.

School began to get better. Most of my teammates liked me, I was popular, and I had a good rapport with the teachers. Not to mention, we were winning basketball games. Coach Daniel spent hours in the gym with me. When I did leave the gym, I would go to the Cochrans' and play basketball with Morris in the evening. Most of the time, Mike, Morris's son, would join us. Mike and I became good friends; I really enjoyed watching him play basketball. He was like a wild animal. I'd get stomach cramps after his games from laughing so much. He was so athletic, but he had no control over his body. He would be on a breakaway and shoot a layup so hard it would bounce back past the three-point line, and he'd run so fast that he couldn't stop. Thank God for the pads behind the goal. They saved his life on more than one occasion.

High school marked many changes in my life. Yet, I was so ashamed of my sexuality; I felt as though I would rather die than face the world or be different from others. Society made me feel unworthy of my own life because my feelings did not emulate society's norm. It was a crazy feeling. Although people considered me the save-all and praised my athletic ability, I still felt unworthy of the life God gave me. I felt completely undeserving of people's friendships as well as God's love, and I was sure no one would ever accept me when I was such a broken mess.

10

No Excuses

"Ninety-nine percent of all failures come from people who have the habit of making excuses."

— *George Washington Carver*

It is much easier to make excuses than to find a way to make our dreams come true. Achieving our dreams means overcoming barriers and challenges. Many would rather give up on their dreams than chase them if chasing involves any self-sacrifice or suffering. In fact, today's generation has made quitting and giving up the norm. We never let our children fail anymore. We might think we are protecting them when we refuse to let them fail, but this isn't true. Failure is a great learning tool. Learning how to pick yourself up and dust yourself off after failure is essential in life. If you ever want to be successful, it is imperative that you learn how to handle failure and find a way to conquer the fear of the unknown.

Many times in my childhood, I elected to endure things that most kids would be too afraid to try. If I really wanted my life to be different, I knew I had to take some chances; even if it meant I had to suffer through some unhappy moments. My best friend Marvin and I had pinky swore as children that our lives would not be like our parents' and that we would make it, come hell or high water.

When I was in middle school, I moved to Monroe, Louisiana, with my grandmother for a year to play five-on-five basketball at Jefferson Upper Elementary School. It was my first time away from home. Home was a small town, where I probably only had six people in my class. Now at Jefferson I had hundreds! I grew up playing six-on-six, and even though I played with my cousins, I needed some organized exposure to this style of play if I ever wanted to make it big. Oklahoma, Iowa, and Kansas were the only states that still played six-on-six basketball. Many kids today don't even know it existed.

In six-on-six, players were not allowed to cross the half court. A team's forwards, or players that shot the ball, were on one side of the court, and their guards would be on the other half guarding the other team's forwards. When the guards rebounded the ball, they would dribble up to half court and throw it to their forwards. Then they'd wait for the other team's guards to rebound and dribble it up to the half court and give them the ball back. I needed more experience playing five-on-five because that's how women's college basketball was played, so I begged my mom to let me move to Louisiana.

I'll never forget my first day of basketball practice there. A little lady named Sonja Hickingbottom was my coach. Her voice sounded more country than mine. I shot a layup, and she yelled, "Let me see you do that again," in a deep southern drawl. I did it. Then she yelled, "Now do it on the other side." So, I did a left-hand layup. "Well I'll be," she cheered. At first, I was struggling to fit in at school. I had never been away from home and believe it or not, I had not been around that many black people in my life. My town was small, and the population was at least seventy-five percent white. After that first day at basketball practice, I knew everything was going to be okay. I knew Mrs. Hickingbottom would look out for me and thank God for her. Without her, I never would have lasted at that school.

It was a seventh- and eighth-grade school. Some of the students there were eighteen years old, some were in detention centers, and the others were gangsters. I had a hard time fitting in. I seemed to stick out like a sore thumb. Thankfully, Mrs. Hickingbottom steered me away from the wrong crowds and took me into her family. Yet, I was scared every day at school. I don't know why because everyone liked the Oklahoma kid who took the team to its one and only 16-0 season. I feel as though I brought hope to some people who didn't have much left. I know I brought some dignity and respect to a school that everyone counted out because of the kind of kids who were enrolled there. I am proud to say I went to Jefferson Upper Elementary.

Throughout my year there, every high school in Monroe was trying to connect with my family to try to get me to go to their school. My grandmother enjoyed the attention, and it felt really good to make her so proud. She was always so kind and gentle with me. She made me feel loved and appreciated, and she made me feel as though the little things I contributed were the highlights of her day. She always called me Crissy Love, and she gave me a feeling that I had never really experienced before. This was something I needed, something I craved. Unconditional love.

All of the other grandchildren hated our relationship. Maybe because she often gave me pocket change to buy candy. It wasn't because I was good at basketball, like most might think, it was because I helped make her life easier. When she got home from work, I had cleaned, washed the dishes, mowed the lawn, and taken out the trash. I never asked her for anything. The other grandkids always had their hands stuck out even though they never tried to help her in any way. But when it came to choosing a new high school, they all got let down. My mother said she missed me too much and made me move back to Oklahoma.

As soon as I moved back to Stringtown, all of the surrounding high schools were trying to get me to come play for them this time. Since I played in another state in my eighth-grade year, I didn't need a transfer letter to play at the school of my choice in Oklahoma. This is when things began to change again; my life got very interesting.

I ended up going to high school in Atoka, not Stringtown. I ended up in Atoka because we found a much better house there. No more rats or holes in the floor for us. Of course, we still brought enough roach eggs with us during the move to still have roaches. Nevertheless, roaches and all, we thought we were living the high life. I didn't want to go to Atoka, but after my mom found a job in the school cafeteria and my dad found a job as a school janitor, I had no say so.

In the end, going to Atoka was the best move for my family and me. Atoka had one of the best high school coaches in the state. Not only was he a great coach, he was an even better person. Phil Daniel took all of my God-given talent and molded me into a great player, all the while pouring his wisdom into me as a person as well.

Today, you see so many athletes who are just that—athletes. Coach Daniel spent hours with me. Basketball was our life. We woke up, practiced from 6 or 7 a.m. with the team, and had our regular practice after school. Late at night we would go to the gym and shoot five hundred shots. Coach Daniel taught me how to think about the game as well as play it. He was always giving me bits of knowledge here and there to increase my basketball IQ. The most important thing he ever taught me was that my mind was just as valuable as my athletic ability. When I was a pro athlete, it was my mind that kept me at elite status rather than my ability.

I decided to give myself the best opportunity to become the best basketball player I could be. I knew basketball was my ticket out of the life I seemed to be stuck in. I took some huge chances with the hope that they would pay off in the end. I knew that if I did not invest into my own future, no one else would either. Just as many people take risks by investing in the stock market, I also took some huge risks to become a better basketball player. In the end, it helped me grow in so many other ways.

I learned to have a greater appreciation for my mother. There were so many nights that I missed my mom while I was in Louisiana. I even missed her yelling, her cursing, and her spankings. My grandmother and my mother both loved me; they just expressed their love for me in different ways. My grandmother was able to love me in a stress-free environment, and my mother loved me amid the chaos that was in our lives. But love is love, and it wasn't until I was older that I realized that.

11

Positive Impact

"A strong, positive mental attitude will create more miracles than any wonder drug."

— *Patricia Neal*

I'll never forget trying out for the USA Select team. I was so nervous that I even tried to find reasons not to go. It was such a big honor and I couldn't dare tell my dad I didn't want to go or that I was scared senseless. I would be competing against some of the best basketball players from around the United States.

I had my athletic director, Donald Parham, to thank for getting me invited to trials. He believed in my ability so much. I was frightened that I wouldn't be able to measure up and that I would be coming home ashamed, with my tail between my legs, because I wasn't good enough. This situation taught me just how powerful the mind can be. I literally lived the statement, "you are what you think you are."

I only knew a couple of girls at this trial. One of those girls was Charlotte Smith from North Carolina; I'd met C-Smith at the Kodak All-American game. While we were there, she graciously allowed me to wear some of her dress clothes to the banquet because I couldn't afford any. She rescued me then, and little did I know, she would soon rescue me again.

I was playing terribly at the tryouts for the USA Basketball team. I looked as though I didn't belong among all of these great players. After all, I was from Atoka, Oklahoma. I was feeling really down on myself, and I kept telling myself, over and over, that I didn't belong there. As I was reiterating all of this to myself, I wandered off the court and headed to a corner. Feeling lonely, ashamed, sorry for myself, and fighting back tears, I finally made my way to that corner. As I was sitting in the corner with tears streaming down my cheeks, Charlotte Smith and Sylvia Crawley walked over to me.

"What's wrong?" C-Smith asked.

"Well, I embarrassed myself, and I don't belong here," I answered.

C-Smith stuck her hand out to me and said, "We think you're the best player here. Come on. You can hang with us."

I instantly felt better. I grabbed C-Smith's hand, and with a smirk creeping back on my face, off we went. I ended up getting MVP of that team too. Maybe Charlotte and Sylvia were correct; maybe I was the best player there. Either way, if they hadn't approached me and stuck out a hand to me, I don't know where I'd be right now.

Charlotte Smith, Sylvia Crawley, and I ended up being lifelong friends. We even ended up playing on the same professional basketball team in the American Basketball League, and they ended up taking care of me then too. They invited me over for dinners and movies; although, I don't think we ever finished a movie. We would always fall asleep well before the movie was over. Charlotte and Sylvia were also a big reason I ended up being Rookie of the Year in that league. I averaged a double-double my first year mainly because of their unselfishness. They told me, "We are going to block our men out, and you get every rebound." I got the credit for those rebounds, but their commitment to winning got me those stats. They affected my life in ways they may never know. I will always feel that they were a key part of the success I experienced during that time. Little did I know that we three would eventually be teammates in the American Basketball League, then rivals in the Women's National Basketball Association. The respect I have for these two women and their ability to affect lives is unparalleled. The leadership, kindness, and humility they showed me influenced me to follow their example.

12

Learning from J.R.

"We learn by example and by direct experience because there are real limits to the adequacy of verbal instruction."

— *Malcolm Gladwell*

Throughout high school, I had a friend named J.R. Cooksey, who was a car dealer. He and I were as opposite as night and day. He was a redneck, wore a mullet, and didn't have an athletic bone in his body. Meanwhile, I was a great athlete, black, and poor as hell. All of his friends were rednecks and always gave him a hard time about having me around because of my skin color. I think at first, J.R. felt sorry for me, but I started growing on him. He always did what he could to look out for me. He let me do odd jobs around the dealership to make some cash when I wasn't at school or in the gym. He let me detail cars, and eventually, he taught me how to put car stereos in. We became great friends. I went everywhere with him—car auctions, auto shows, you name it, I was with him. He was definitely one of the angels God sent to me.

J.R. had a big heart, he truly cared about people. But he also had a slick tongue and a dirty mouth. Everyone judged him on that, but I didn't mind it at all. J.R. became one of my biggest fans, and during my college years, he never missed a game. No matter how far he had to drive, he was always there.

I learned a lot about responsibility through our friendship. He trusted me with the cars on his lot as well as the safety of his children. I respected J.R. so much because he took a lot of criticism from his friends for constantly having the black kid around. They couldn't believe he put his trust in me. He never judged me, and he always treated me with love and respect no matter what other people thought. He didn't care that I was poor, and he didn't care that I was black. He never judged me like most of the other people in my community did. He only cared that I was honest, treated others with respect, and always kept my word. He judged me by my actions rather than my skin color, socioeconomic status, or what other people thought about me. I believe he did this because he also knew what it felt like to be judged by others. People had always formed erroneous opinions about him because of his appearance and his slick tongue. We were completely different, but at the same time, we were kindred spirits. We put our faith into each other and built a friendship, a friendship that would last a lifetime.

Sometimes it only takes a helping hand to lift us up. I've had many helping hands throughout my life, and I've had to be just as willing to accept the help as the helpers were to extend it.

Many times in today's world, people who accept help from others are viewed as weak, and therefore, many will not accept the help that others offer. Yet in reality, it takes great strength to trust someone enough to let them into your life and even more to lend a helping hand. It is important to look out for the kindness and welcome kindness when it comes. Inviting the right kind of kindness into your life can completely change your life's direction. And yet, these days, you have to be careful of accepting someone's kindness, because the world is not always a kind place anymore. Don't just accept kindness blindly from anyone. Be selective so you can prevent horrible situations. Sadly, people use each other for gain. But inviting the right kind of kindness can completely change the direction of your life. And that is what happened to me many times over. You just have to be choosy.

13

More Lessons from Baseball

*"Baseball is almost the only orderly
thing in a very unorderly world. If you
get three strikes, even the best lawyer
in the world can't get you off."*

— *Bill Veeck*

Without realizing it, I was constantly making choices
that set me apart from other girls, and other people.
I played baseball as much for the love of the game
as I did to prove to myself and others that I could
do it. It gave me lots of confidence heading into the
unknown territory of defining my sexuality. I knew
it would be a tough, hard road to travel, but it was
better than the alternative. It is also a part of my life
that I still have a difficult time accepting. I don't have
a hard time accepting it because an imperfect society
tells me it's wrong. No, I battled with my sexuality

because my religion said I was going to go to hell. I had a hard time understanding this because God still created me, and God doesn't make mistakes.

Throughout my early life I had this inner battle with how the church and God viewed me. I have been searching for the answers around my faith and sexuality since I discovered who I am. I only know that I've felt as though I've been preparing myself for something all of my life. When it comes down to it, I offer no excuses for who I am.

In my sophomore and junior years in high school I played on the boys' baseball team. There was no girls' softball team, so the boys' coach, who coached against me for years in little league, asked me to play. Without hesitation, I accepted his offer. I never had a problem fitting in there. I had played against all of these guys in little league, so they knew I could play. I was a relief pitcher and a designated hitter for our catcher half of the season during my sophomore year. I almost always had the best slugging percentage and I didn't strike out often. I may not have hit with a lot of power, but I always put the ball in play, and had great control. I could hit behind a runner or pull the ball if the coach wanted me to. I was a place hitter.

I remember one specific game from high school baseball. We were playing a team from Asher, Oklahoma. They had a kid who was pitching in the mid-nineties, but he had major control issues. He would throw a strike one pitch, and then the next pitch would go over the backstop. That was a scary thing for a batter. Having a pitcher throw a ninety-mile-an-hour fastball at you when he had no idea where the pitch was going when it left his hand was frightening. All he had to do was hit one batter, and everyone else was scared senseless. Once, we even saw him break a kid's wrist. After that, most of my teammates were so scared that they either swung or ran from most of his pitches. We played this team in a doubleheader that day. The kid who typically started at second base for us was late getting to a game, so I started in his spot. I was the only person on the team who got a hit off of that pitcher that day. Actually, I got two hits, and turned a couple of double plays. Needless to say, Asher killed us both games, but that was my breakout game.

Curtis Inge, our coach, started putting me on the mound. I could throw junk pitches, but I wasn't just blowing the ball by batters. Later, I figured out that he did it to either save our star pitcher's arm or to mess with the batters psychologically. None of those guys wanted to be struck out by a girl. They would put so much pressure on themselves and get so worried about being teased that they'd get in their own heads and strike out anyway.

I played baseball to prove to myself and everyone else that I could compete with anyone at anything that I put my mind to. I didn't use the fact that I was a girl as an excuse not to try something. I also never allowed what others thought about me playing baseball bother me. Baseball gave me, as well as many others, some great memories. When I was inducted into the Oklahoma Sports Hall of Fame, the Chickasaw Nation governor walked over to me and asked me to come take a picture with his son. I had struck out his son once in a high school game, and he remembered me. We had some great laughs about that while we were taking pictures.

We've all been equipped with the ability to achieve just about anything we want to, as long as we are willing to pay the price. I was teased, called names, and frowned upon for playing a sport that I grew up loving, but I was more than willing to pay the price. I am certain now that the memories I made playing that sport were well worth it.

14

Forgiveness

*"The weak can never forgive. Forgiveness is
the attribute of the strong."*

— *Mahatma Gandhi*

When I was in the third grade, my father started teaching me, or should I say training me, never to accept less than my best. He subconsciously instilled in me that mediocrity was not for me.

My father's way of teaching me this lesson, though, always crushed me. All I wanted was for him to be proud of me. He never told me that I had done a good job or even acted like I was doing something spectacular. There weren't many kids competing at the levels that I was competing or playing against older-grade kids like I was. I was doing things on the court that kids my age and older weren't able to do. I had some forty- and fifty-point games at that age, but he still never told me that I was doing a good job. I never knew that he was bragging to his friends or that he was even at my games. He tended to pace around like a nervous freak; I never really saw him at my games unless he was drunk and causing a scene.

It wasn't until I was older that I realized that he was always training me to give more and constantly strive to be better and do better. His lessons taught me never to focus on the things I did well. I learned never to accept complacency, even if I was the best player on my team, but to focus on improving the weaker points in my game.

My father also taught me to try to always be the best at whatever I decided to do. He was the school janitor and would often come home saying that he had the shiniest floors in our town. Once, I smarted off and said, "That's something to be proud of." He grabbed me by the arm, put his hand on my chin, and made me look him right in the eye, and he said, "It doesn't matter what kind of job you have, you need to be the best at whatever it is you are doing at the time. Do all of your work with pride, and people will respect you for it." Those words have stuck with me in everything I do. My father and I didn't have many moments like that, so I really took it to heart when stuff like that happened.

My mother may have drunk lots of beer, but she worked her tail off too. When I was a kid, I hated it when she came to my games. She yelled so loudly that it embarrassed me. I never had to wonder if she was at my games because I could always hear her when she was. If I missed a free throw, she would yell, "Why the hell do you think they call them free throws?" Needless to say, I quickly became a great free-throw shooter, I didn't want to hear her yelling that at my games. I could block out everyone at the gym except for my mom. As I mentioned earlier, my mom and dad, who met at Murray State College, in Tishomingo, Oklahoma, were college All-Americans themselves and stars on their basketball teams. It was safe to say that basketball was in my genes; I was born to play that game.

Unless she was drinking, Mama always seemed to be in a bad mood. That was very hard to grasp when I was a kid. Now, though, I know and understand. Being responsible for five kids, working two jobs, and taking care of the house was seriously stressing her out. She never really got a break from us, so beer was her only release. Her kids were her life, and she did the best she could to provide for us. She loved us more than she loved herself.

I'll never forget; I was probably in the third or fourth grade when Mama was arrested for stealing food for us to eat. She stole and wrote a hot check to try and provide for us. I had to peel my sisters and brothers off of her when the cops picked her up. I told Mama, "Don't worry. I'll take care of them." I had no idea when she was coming back, all I knew was that we were going to be staying with our grandparents until she returned. I got my brothers and sisters ready for school each day, and my grandparents cooked for us. My grandfather ended up selling some of his cattle to pay her bail. I still don't know all of the details of what happened; all I know was that we got our mother back.

It wasn't until I left home that I realized what an amazing woman my mother was. I was almost twenty-five years old when I really learned to appreciate her struggle. I learned to make sense of my life too. I realized that my mother was one of the hardest working people I'd ever seen. One of the greatest qualities that I learned from her was, "No one gives you anything; if you want something, you work hard and get it."

When it came to discipline, my mother always followed through. I even thought that she just enjoyed whipping my older brother and me. Now, I know that we deserved those whippings; we were just some bad little hooligans. My mom taught me that there would always be consequences for my actions. Life doesn't care why you made a poor decision or if you were sorry for what you did. The consequences are coming regardless. This, by far, is the most important lesson that those whippings taught me.

My mother also taught me that I am still not any better than anyone else no matter how high I climb in life. She taught me that God looks at us all the same and does not give anyone special preference. She also taught me that life does not discriminate, and it can deal anyone hard blows. One minute you can be well off, and the next, you can be really poor. You never know when you will be on the bad side of life. So it is important to be careful how you treat people who are less fortunate, because at any time, you could be on the whipping end of life. My mother insisted that we treat people the way we want to be treated, and she refused to accept anything less.

My mother constantly baffled me. I felt that she could be cruel at times, but then, on the other hand, I knew that she would give her last dime to someone she felt needed it more. As I look back on my life, I now realize that my parents taught me a lot of good things amidst the chaos that was going on in our home. My parents were good-hearted, loving, protecting, and caring people, but I did not see this as a young girl. I was only focused on all the things I considered bad about them and the life they gave their children.

It took many years for me to realize that God had put me on a specific path. A path where He put everything I needed to learn and grow from. Some of those things were good, and some of those things were bad. However, they were all put there to give me the strength and courage I needed to become what He intended me to be. I find that, for the most part, we create our own problems as we become adults. Most of the problems in our paths are there because we sometimes make bad decisions.

I was twenty-five when I let go of the anger I felt towards my parents. I finally realized that hate and anger only hurt the person who is holding on to it. I'm pretty certain that I never voiced my feelings to my parents. It didn't bother them that I had all of these negative emotions bottled up inside me because I never talked about it.

I finally learned that forgiveness is the key to a calm soul. I did not want to feel miserable inside anymore. I stopped trying to rationalize my childhood. I realized that even if I could get some kind of legitimate reasons for their actions, those reasons would never change the things that I had experienced. So instead, I decided to focus on the lessons I learned from the incidents that I had perceived as negatives in my life. I felt as though I had two options: one, I could continue to dwell on the past and let those bad feelings consume me; or two, I could just plain and simply let it go.

Deciding to let go gave my parents and me a second chance. They were not the best parents in the world when we were kids, but there is no doubt in my mind that they loved us very seriously. Once I learned to forgive, I started to see all of the good things my parents had taught me.

Who do you need to forgive to allow your life to move forward? Forgiving releases its owner from the mayhem this emotion creates in his soul. The lack of forgiveness leads to hate. Because the two are so closely related, we don't recognize when the former turns into the latter. Hate destroys the owner from the inside. Allowing hate to dwell in your soul makes it easier to hate other things, and before you know it, your life revolves around it, and you're controlled by that miserable feeling you've allowed to linger and grow.

Hate literally can be equated to a severe infection in the body. Anyone who has been sick with a bad infection knows how good the relief feels once the infection is terminated.

Love is like an antibiotic for hate. We all have to decide what we want in life and plot a course to that destination. We also need to realize that we can't carry all of our hurtful baggage for some destinations. To make the trip easier, some things need to be left at home in the drawers or lost somewhere in a forgotten place.

To heal, we need to develop the courage and strength to release old negative feelings that slow us down and clutter up our path. Negative emotions only make us stay in a miserable place of comfort.

Negative past baggage distorts us from learning new things and prevents us from soaring to the highest mountaintops. The baggage-free love you give to others shines on them like a warm summer day.

15

Adventures with Marvin

"The worst part of holding the memories is not the pain. It's the loneliness of it. Memories need to be shared."

— *Lois Lowry*

The older I've gotten, the more I have realized that happiness is truly a choice. I have learned through trial and error that our happiness can be what we make it. We can either dwell on our problems and shortcomings or we can do something about them. Each of us can choose to take the positive aspects from the negative events that life hurls at us.

Instead of dwelling on hurtful pasts, we should try to remember the good and use everything else as instruments of growth. Personally, I choose to view the bad things in my life as necessary lessons that helped me develop into the person I am today. I now also choose to focus on the good in my life.

My brothers, cousins, and I were a handful as kids. At times we were similar to a band of wild children. Each of us was typically armed with some kind of weapon: pellet guns, BB guns, machetes, knives, rocks, or other homemade weapons. Since we didn't have much money, we lived off of the land. We hunted rabbit, squirrel, raccoon, and deer. My mother had this rule: if you killed it, you eat it. So whenever we killed any of these animals, we cleaned them, and often ate them for dinner.

During the summers, we ate a lot of fish because we fished so much. We had fun wading in the creeks and rivers while we fished. We fished for crappies, bass, and catfish. I hate to admit it, but Marvin was the master fisherman. He really could fish, plus, he had the steadiest hand I have ever seen. He could put a toothpick in the barrel of his pellet gun and shoot a locust in a tree. I was the one who would climb up there and get the locust, and then we'd fill up a jar. Once we had enough, we would use them as bait and fish with them.

One day, as Marvin and I were hunting in the woods, we happened upon a creek. Before I left the house, my mother said, "If you come home wet and ashy, I'm gonna beat your ass." Whippings were nothing to me at this point. I was pretty tough. Plus, I always wore an extra pair of shorts under my pants. This helped relieve the sting of the whippings. Once we saw the creek, I looked at Marvin and said, "I bet I can jump that creek." He looked at me and said, "Girl, you can't jump that creek." I backed up at least the length of a basketball court, rocked from the ball of my foot to the heel, and took off. I was at top speed about halfway through, so by the time I got to the water, I was spent. I jumped as hard as I could and sailed through the air. Suddenly, though, the sailing stopped. A big splash, along with Marvin's laughter, was all you heard. The water was over my head, and I was completely soaked.

I dog paddled to the bank and pulled myself out. "Girl, I told you, you could not jump over that creek," Marvin said. "Now, I know I can't because I tried," I replied. I took my wet clothes off and started hanging them on the trees. I stripped all the way down to my underwear; Marvin couldn't stop laughing. Next thing you know, I was chasing him through the woods in my panties—no shoes, no socks. I jumped on his back and tackled him.

"Stop laughing," I yelled in his face.

"Get off me," he yelled back.

We rolled around on the ground and cracked up laughing. We backtracked and got our guns and looked for rabbits to shoot. For most of the day, I was rabbit hunting in my underwear, making sure to give my clothes plenty of time to dry. We shot three rabbits that day. At the end of the day we went back to the creek to get my clothes. I got dressed, then we cleaned the rabbits and headed home.

As soon as I walked into the house, somehow, my mom knew that I had been wet. She came over, grabbed my arm, and yelled, "Didn't I tell your little black ass not to get wet?" I now know how she knew. My wrinkly clothes and ashy skin gave me away. (For those of you who don't know what ash is, it is the gray color the skin turns after getting wet before lotion is applied.) "Get in that room," she yelled.

Mama went and got her belt. I knew what was coming next. Usually, she grabbed me by the arm, and I danced around and yelled, "Ooh," "Ahh," and "Ouch" like it was hurting. It did hurt a little, but the shorts I had on under my pants buffered the pain. For some reason, my mother noticed the shorts this time. She ordered me to strip naked and lay on the bed on my stomach. I did as I was told. She then whipped me from the bottom of my feet to the back of my head. I tried hard not to cry, but that whipping hurt like no other.

Even though it hurt, it did not stop me from being a wild child. As kids, we often woke up early and left the house, but we always returned before the sun went down. We knew if we didn't, that was an automatic whipping.

Marvin and my brother Gerald each had a Shetland pony. I rode my brother's horse the most because everyone else was scared of him. He'd run off with anyone he could sense was afraid of him. My cousins, who came from the city, would get the ride of their lives. When I put them on that horse, he'd take off and didn't stop until I could get a hold of the reins.

Shetland ponies have really tough mouths. They would ride the reins hard, and still wouldn't stop. Marvin and I rode those ponies to the café in Stringtown and tied them up out back just like in the old Western movies. I can't remember the name of the owners of the Stringtown Café, but I do remember they were good people. They created a whole menu for us. They had nickel soft drinks, twenty-five cent pickles, and they even created burger discounts for us. We would tie our ponies up out back, go into the café, throw our nickel on the counter, and get a little cup of Coke. We'd always get a pickle to go, to share it on our pony ride back home. It felt as though we were in the western movies where guys would run into the saloon, get a stiff drink then ride away on their horses. Marvin and I had so many adventures that I cannot write about them all. We were basically Huck Finn and Tom Sawyer.

I think I could write a second book about the adventures of two little country black kids that would leave people laughing and shaking their heads at the same time. He was the brains, and I was the brawn; meaning, he had most of the crazy ideas, and I had the guts to put them into effect. He usually sat back and watched and laughed at me as I attempted something remarkably stupid. I'm pretty sure that during our childhood we tried everything from dog milk to snails. At least I did anyway. I know it sounds really nasty, but come on, we lived in a town with about three hundred people. We had to manufacture our own fun and excitement.

Randall was Marvin's cousin. Their dads were brothers. Randall lived with his grandmother, and they lived right beside our grandparents. He had a huge family. His grandmother had twelve boys and two girls. Randall was the same age as Marvin and me, and every day we would convince him to come play with us. We would always cook up some big scheme to get him with. We did this every day, and every day he came back as though he had no idea the joke would again be on him.

Randall had lived in Oklahoma City most of his life, and he knew nothing about country life. Once, when he came over, I looked at Marvin and said, "Watch this." We had this old hen that had some baby chicks. She was meaner than a raccoon that had been locked in a cage for three days. It was a sport for me. I knew if you got too close to those chicks that the old hen would chase you. I did it all the time. I provoked the hen into chasing me while Marvin sat and watched and laughed. So I decided that I would bet Randall that he wasn't fast enough to catch one of those baby chicks. He looked at me and dashed after one. He caught the chick, looked at me, and said, "See I told you I could catch it." Little did he know that the fun was just beginning.

About that time, the old mama hen ruffled up her feathers and started chasing after Randall. She flew up on his head and started flogging and pecking him. He started running and screaming with the old hen perched all over his head and shoulders. Marvin and I were on the ground laughing so hard, we caught cramps in our sides. This went on for what seemed like minutes, so I finally yelled, "Drop the baby chick, and she'll stop." That old hen whipped Randall like he was her son. He finally dropped the chick, but he kept running. The hen flew to the ground, and Randall ran into his grandma's house. We knew he was going to tattle on us. Still dying of laughter, we quickly ran into Marvin's grandma's house. Everyone wanted to know what was so funny. We told everyone the story and Marvin's grandma gave us a few choice words. She told us that what we did wasn't funny, and that we'd better leave Randall alone. To this day, Randall still gets angry when we tell this story, and he's still terrified of chickens.

16

Playing With Fire

"I never smoked a cigarette until I was nine."

— *H.L. Mencken*

Marvin and I would sometimes catch crawdads and badger my mom or his grandmother until they fried them for us. We liked to catch them, clean them, and store them in the freezer until we had enough to fry. One day, we did not want to wait on my mom or his grandmother, so we decided to sneak a skillet, some cornmeal, some Crisco, some seasonings, and a cigarette lighter out of the house. Some of the stuff came from my house and some came from grandma's, but we rounded up all the supplies we needed. Since we could not cook, we recruited his sister Donna to cook the crawdads for us. She was a few years older and in the eighth grade. We were pretty proud of ourselves for actually sneaking all of the materials out to cook, but we never took into account that it was a ridiculously dry summer.

Marvin and I got the crawdads and dropped them in a bucket of water while Donna got the fire started, filled the skillet full of oil, and mixed the spices in the cornmeal. Everything was going great. We caught what we thought were enough crawdads. So we quit fishing, started separating the tail from the body, and began cleaning them while Donna started frying them. We were eating them straight out of the hot grease. We were eating crawdad tails as though we hadn't eaten in a few days. Not only were we burning the tips of our fingers, we had severely scorched tongues.

We were almost halfway through our feast when it happened. The grass caught a spark and the flames began to soar on this hot Indian summer day. We had started the biggest grass fire in our childhood. When the fire started, we began trying to stomp it out. Marvin and I were stomping as though our lives depended on it, then his pant leg caught on fire. Suddenly, we had to take our focus off the fire to put his pant leg out. As we were trying to keep Marvin from going up in smoke, Donna decided to pour the crawdad water on the fire. What a huge mistake. She threw that water on the hot grease, and any chance we had of saving our backsides and putting out the fire went up in smoke with the rest of the pasture. At that point, there was nothing to do but run away as fast as we could.

By the time we got close to home, my grandfather had already spotted the smoke. The fire was so bad the cows started running through the fences to escape. There wasn't anything funny about this incident at the time; we were actually frightened. We all accepted the fact that our butts were about to be just as scorched as our tongues. I can't even describe to you the whipping my mother gave me. I never again risked getting a whipping for playing with fire again. Now, looking back, we laugh about this story to this day while we argue about whose fault the fire was.

I remember my first encounter with cigarettes, thanks to my cousin Donna. Donna asked me if I wanted to smoke. I decided to partake as I always wondered what it was like. Both of my parents smoked and even though I hated the smell, they made it look so cool. Donna wasn't old enough to buy or smoke cigarettes, she was only about twelve. This didn't stop her though. She started sneaking into purses or picking up someone's pack after they laid it down. Donna was the best at sneaking the things she wanted out of the house. All I had to do was ask her mother some questions to distract her, and Donna could get whatever she wanted. Her plan worked like a charm every time. So, we used this plan and got the cigarettes. However, we didn't know where we were going to go to smoke them without getting caught. Then I had the bright idea to go to the chicken house. I figured no one would ever catch us in there, and no one would be able to see our smoke. My dad always entertained us by making smoke rings, so I was dying to try to make rings out of my own smoke. Once I mastered it, I would show all of my cousins; I was picturing their jealousy already.

We went to the chicken house, got our cigarettes lit, and had only taken a couple puffs when my grandfather opened the door. We were like deer in headlights. The fight-or-flight response never even triggered. We were stone cold busted. Apparently, my cousin Stephan saw us go into the chicken house and went and told my granddad. He thought we were in there getting his eggs to go cook, and since our last cooking incident cost him his hay, he came to check on us. I'm pretty sure he was happier to see us with cigarettes between our fingers than he would have been seeing us with eggs in our hands. All I could do was pray he would make us put the cigarettes out and let it go. Shoot, he could have even disciplined us himself, but he had to go and tell my mom.

My mother made me smoke a half pack of cigarettes and swallow the smoke. She wanted me to inhale it, but since I didn't really know how to do that, I swallowed it. In hindsight, I think my granddad wished he would have just spanked me and let it go because I know he didn't enjoy the punishment my mother doled out. That moment and that amount of throwup will always be fresh in my mind. I hate cigarettes to this day. This memory is burned into my mind forever. No pun intended.

17

College Life at Southeastern Oklahoma State

*"If you don't like something, change it.
If you can't change it, change your attitude."*

— *Maya Angelou*

The process of deciding on Southeastern Oklahoma State University after returning from Louisiana Tech began with numerous conversations with Cindy and Morris. They had both attended school there, and my cousin Jeff also went there for college. Cindy and Morris wanted me to at least visit the university. I visited out of respect for them, but I had no intention of enrolling there. First of all, they were an NAIA school. Secondly, I lived about thirty miles from this school, and I never knew it existed. Thirdly, that school had the worst women's basketball team in the world. Despite all of these things, I visited because I knew it would make Cindy and Morris happy.

During my visit, I met the athletic director Dr. Parham. I also met the women's basketball coach, Nick Keith. They were both very nice people and I enjoyed meeting with them. They made me feel really comfortable. They became a part of my everyday life during the recruiting process. Honestly, I don't think anyone courted me as hard as they did. I almost got sick of them. I started watching some of the women's basketball games, but they were awful. Not to mention, there were only about sixty people at the games, and none of them looked like they were students at Southeastern.

As time went on, Dr. Parham and I talked about a lot of things. We talked about how I could improve the program, how I could bring some recognition to our part of the state, and how funny it was that he and I both came from Atoka. How could that not be destiny? Despite all of my earlier reservations, I decided to go to Southeastern.

All of my life, it seemed as though everyone around me depended on me. I learned to fill big shoes at a very young age; at least it felt that way. I had started playing competitive basketball in the third grade. I started on the fifth- and sixth-grade team, and I felt it was up to me to make sure we all had success. I knew joining the athletic program at Southeastern would be no different. Plus, let's be real, these kinds of challenges were right up my ally. I knew my shoulders were big enough to carry the load.

Choosing to transfer to Southeastern Oklahoma State University turned out to be one of the better decisions I have made in my life. It allowed me to build a huge network of friends and learn more about myself and my family, and it brought my best friend Marvin back into my life.

Dr. Parham, the athletic director at Southeastern, became a major part of my life. He always had this cigar in his mouth. He never smoked it though. He just chewed on it. He always told me jokes that I never really got, but I laughed anyway. He treated me like I was one of his children. He also checked on my classes and constantly made sure I took the right steps and made the right moves to graduate college. If I was slacking off in my classes, he would sit me down in his office and give me an earful. He became my biggest fan but not just a basketball fan; he became a fan of me as a person.

Dr. Parham put a lot of time, energy, and effort into women's basketball while I was at Southeastern. We did our jobs on the court, so that made it a lot easier for him to go up the hill to fight for money for our program. We were an extraordinarily balanced team. We had some individually talented players, and together, we worked like a well-oiled engine. We all understood our roles, but I think the biggest thing that made our team work so well was my unwillingness to be a superstar. I never wanted the credit. In games where I had to score thirty or more points to win, I did just that. But in games that I could give my teammates the opportunity to shine, I let them shine. That way everyone was happy. No one ever felt jealousy or resentment when I had to take games over to guarantee a win for our team.

My sophomore year in college marked a lot of

change in my life. Marvin lived in Ada and attended East Central University, only about an hour away, so I saw him often. He spent most of his time with his girlfriend, Debbie, who he eventually married and is still married to today. I think being able to see Marvin regularly brought some peace back to my life. It reminded me of when we were kids and helped me escape from the pressure I was under. My sophomore year was also the year I made my first USA Basketball team. Making this team set me up for the future. It got my name out there and really gave me the opportunity to prove myself. Every opportunity I was given to show people what I could do, I capitalized on it.

I got really comfortable by the time I was a junior at Southeastern. I had become close to my college coach and Nick, the women's basketball coach, a funny little white-haired man who loved golf. I pulled all sorts of pranks on him throughout my college career. I even scared him on many occasions. Once while we were on a trip playing a relatively important game, I pretended that I fell down some stairs and couldn't walk. I could have gotten an Emmy or something for this performance. I had cried real tears and everything. I went the whole nine yards. I'm sure Nick was worried about my health, but I'm one hundred percent sure he was thinking, "Oh my God, this can't be happening." I let him worry for a while then I sprang to my feet and told him I was joking. He turned so red I could see his blood pressure rising. I was definitely the team clown.

It wasn't until my junior and senior year that I started to come into my own as a basketball player.

I played pick-up with the men's team, and I found a game at the rec whenever I could. Basketball officially became an obsession for me during my junior and senior years. I realized how life and basketball correlated. I realized how hard work could help you achieve any goal you set for yourself; that's when I fully understood that basketball was my ticket in life. Up until my junior year, basketball had been something that I felt I was just gifted with. Later, it turned out to be a skill that I had a burning desire to be the best at. I didn't know where my talent was going to take me, but I knew it was going to take me somewhere.

My senior year of college seemed to fly by. It marked the year that I accomplished the one thing I am most proud of. I was going to graduate from Southeastern. Similar to me, both of my parents attended college, both of my parents were college All-Americans, and both of my parents had the talent to be whatever they wanted to be. But neither of my parents graduated from college. I had the opportunity of being the first person in my family to graduate college. It was so rewarding to set that example for my three younger brothers and sisters. Both my sisters later graduated college. B.J. is a drug and alcohol counselor, Brandi is a small Bank of America manager, and my younger brother Gerald works in the oil field, making great money. I choose to believe that I set a precedent in my family, influencing my siblings to follow suit. Earning my diploma and graduating college was key to helping break the cycle in my family.

I could not believe that college had come and gone

by so quickly. My family was proud of me, but Dr. Parham was even prouder. Graduation is the accomplishment he really wanted for me. This was his dream. He wanted me to graduate even more than he wanted me to win MVP awards. I did not want to walk during graduation, but Dr. Parham insisted. He knew this was going to be a moment that I would remember forever.

18

Life in the Pros

*"To dream anything you want to dream,
that's the beauty of mankind. To do anything
you want to do, that's the strength of human
will. To trust yourself to test your limits,
that's the courage to succeed."*

— *Bernard Edmonds*

What's it really like to be a professional athlete?
Everyone recognizes the endorsement deals, the
games on television, and the nice cars. Yet, few
people really understand the extremely hard work,
stress, sacrifice, and sleep deprivation that comes
with being a professional athlete. I'm not looking
for sympathy for professional athletes. Every professional athlete chooses this path. I am, however,
trying to give readers a realistic window into this
world.

The games that fans watch only tell half the story. Quite frankly, fans only get to see the finished product. Fans do not know about the insane number of hours a professional athlete puts into their craft, nor do they see the tremendous amount of time athletes spend away from their friends and family. Professional athletes sacrifice their life for the love of their sport. The lifestyle is so difficult that only three percent of the population can mentally, physically, and emotionally push themselves to this level of greatness.

In this rigorous lifestyle, there's no off-season. In fact, to be great is a kind of sickness in itself, almost a disease afflicting a few. Friends, family, and life come second to a professional athlete's craft. Not only do athletes work hard to improve their craft, but they also have numerous off-court responsibilities. Team appearances, public speaking engagements, endorsement deal engagements, and anything else the team decides the athlete needs to do, are all part of the agreement. Thus, the phrase "to whom much is given, much is expected" applies to professional athletes.

Needless to say, free time is a very valuable commodity for professional athletes, and most of them guard their free time fiercely. Fans tend to interpret this as rude or cocky, but it's usually not that at all. Imagine a scenario where you work all day and have the stress of losing your job, or just had a bad day at work. Then you attempt to head home, and five thousand people want to stop you for an autograph. All the while, you promised your own daughter, who you see sparingly, that you would be home by a certain time to take her to a movie. How patient would you be?

I was never that famous, but I spent plenty of time with people who were. I dealt with this inconvenience by making myself so accessible that I was never a big deal. I often ate with fans and stayed after games to sign as many autographs as possible. I felt it was never a big deal when fans saw me. I never wanted to be famous, nor did I ever consider myself famous.

Personally, I feel like the moment you put yourself on a pedestal, you begin setting yourself up for failure. We are all just humans, some of us with more privileges than others, but we are not objects to be idolized.

Professional athletes are people with extraordinary talents, but at their core, they are just like you. They come with expiration dates, and they fall short more than most because they encounter significant temptations that most never face. The difference is that when professional athletes make a mistake, the whole world gets to watch them fall while ordinary people's mistakes are played out in private. Why would anyone envy this?

Should athletes be role models? The answer to that question will always be yes, but athletes are and will always be humans. Falling short is something we will always do. That's why I never lost sight of the fact that being a professional athlete was what I did as a profession; it was never who I was as a person.

I went from being a college senior who had no clue what I would do after basketball to being drafted in the eighth round of the American Basketball League.

I wasn't remotely ready for the challenges professional sports had in store for me. I had no idea what to expect, and it was a steep learning curve.

Sheryl Estes with the Colorado Xplosion told me she drafted me because I was the best NAIA player she had ever encountered. Yet, I felt inadequate when it happened. I seemed to have forgotten that I was courted by every college in the country, successfully played on USA Basketball teams, and accumulated every honor my new professional teammates had achieved. But even after all of those accomplishments, I still suffered from a feeling of inferiority. I didn't know what to expect, and I was a little frightened. Yet, I did know the game of basketball like the back of my hand. If I wasn't ready, I would be by the time I got to Colorado. Little did I know, success and money were about to change, and so was my view of a game I loved with all of my heart.

Professional sports forced me to change my view of basketball. I got a quick lesson in the money-talks-and-BS-walks department. That's the first thing professional athletes learn. It's a lesson that has a positive and a negative side. You learn quickly that the more money you earn, the more responsibility you have. Shooters are expected to make shots, scorers are expected to score, and great defenders are expected to successfully defend. It's a pretty simple thing, really. If you don't accomplish your job to the highest standards, the team will find someone else who can. There is no more, "If the team loses, we all lose." In the pros, if the team loses it's because you did not do your job or earn your keep. When you are in the pros, you have a job to do. No one cares about excuses. Team owners predominately care about winning, losing, and athletes earning their salary.

Since I came from Southeastern Oklahoma State University, a small NAIA college, no one was expecting big things from me. I was definitely not considered one of the best players on my new pro team. But, for some reason, when I was drafted, I felt the weight of the world falling on my shoulders. No one else's expectations of me were very high. However, the expectations that I had put on myself were much higher than anyone could ever have placed on me. My expectations and standards were all that mattered. Most people didn't know I had decided long ago that I would never try to live up to anyone else's expectations. I was only going to live up to my own.

My first year in the pros started with no assumptions, but two important elements combined to change all that. First, my team greatly underestimated my competitive desire; and second, I was reunited with Sylvia Crawley and Charlotte Smith from USA Basketball. They were two of the best teammates I could have ever asked for, and because of their unselfishness, my career flourished. They pulled me aside before a game one day and told me their strategy, "We are going to block our men out and you rebound the basketball." Winning was their number-one priority; they were largely unconcerned with who got the credit.

Although I don't remember many of the games that first year, I do remember that we made the play-offs. Most of all, I remember that I played with one of the best distributors, one of the smartest players, and one of the best people the game of basketball has ever known—Debbie Black.

Debbie was a five-foot-three point guard who played in Australia before the American Basketball League (ABL) and the Women's National Basketball Association (WNBA) were formed. Her nickname, because of her intense tenacity, was the Tasmanian Devil. Her determination will probably never be matched. In all of my years of playing the game of basketball, I've never seen anyone play all out and full speed for forty minutes, without ever looking tired, like Debbie Black did. Her determination, intensity, focus, and will to win were unparalleled. I knew I could never play at her exact pace, but she taught me everything I know about never giving up, leaving it all on the floor, and never saying never. Most importantly, watching how she played the game reinforced my belief that I should never let anyone define me. I learned to not only exceed others' expectations but also to surpass my own.

While I was absorbing Debbie's recipe for success, Sylvia and Charlotte became my family away from family. They taught this little country hick girl how to dress better, and even fed me home-cooked meals from time to time. During my first year in the pros, I averaged eighteen points, ten rebounds, and was named the New Pro Athlete of the Year. They did not give a Rookie of the Year award because all of us were basically rookies in the first year that the league started. My new award brought with it some very positive actions along with some distinctly negative features.

It was really positive because I could get a salary

increase, plus my name was being tossed around with the best players in the country. It also helped me land a shoe deal and obtain a real agent—not one with a side job as a traveling singer. The negative result was that now everyone's expectations of me were outrageous. I had to find a way to outdo a double-double season to be considered successful. Anything less would be considered failure, at least in my eyes.

The amount of pressure I was putting on myself was genuinely crushing. I was no longer playing basketball to try to forget my problems, nor was I playing for fun. I was playing for my livelihood and pride. Once I began playing the game that I had loved for money and pride, its meaning changed for me.

I did not want to embarrass my family or myself on national TV, nor did I want my family ever to pick up the newspapers and read about my failures. Being a professional athlete was not good enough for me; I wanted to excel. I wanted to be important to my team, but I quickly learned that the kind of attention that comes along with being the best is pressure at its peak. At this moment, I realized that God had probably given me so many trials and tribulations in my early years simply to prepare me for this moment. All of the incidents that I had viewed as negatives in my life now gave me the shoulders I needed to thrive as a professional athlete. I had learned early in life to face defeat head on. I already knew how to persevere and make decisions under pressure and in volatile situations. For the first time, I thanked God for allowing me to experience each negative situation I had in my past. All of those incidents combined together taught me the true essence of leadership with humbleness of heart as the main ingredient.

I only played one and a half more years in the ABL. Unfortunately, the ABL went bankrupt in 1998; and then the stakes got higher. When the ABL went under, the WNBA added a special draft to add ABL players to the pool of college seniors. I was under the impression that I was going to be the tenth overall pick and heading to Phoenix for the WNBA. I'd had several discussions with Cheryl Miller and was really excited about the possibility of playing for such a legend.

The pre-draft camp was not so good for me. I was overweight and had volunteered to play the four position (forward) because there were not enough post players at the camp. I was considered one of the best two shooting guards who were attending the camp, but no one was able to see me play my position. Later, I found out that the New York Liberty's general manager forcefully requested to see me at my natural position; she even asked them to match me up against the other shooting guard.

Every WNBA coach was front and center for this match up. It was the last game of camp, and the intensity was cranked up. I ended up putting on the camp's best performance; so good in fact, that Cheryl Miller almost tackled me on the court. She tipped her hand that she wanted to draft me, so New York decided to take me as the sixth overall pick. This was probably the most talented draft in the history of the WNBA; it was the first and only time pros and college players would be pooled together in the same draft. This also was the last time I changed agents;

marking another milestone in my career.

My involvement with the WNBA also allowed me to start playing basketball in Europe, which was a godsend. I experienced different cultures, different family structures, as well as less pressure. Europeans place intense focus on family. They rarely spend their time wishing for fancy cars, big houses, or status. Everyone's intention was to save money to enjoy a big family vacation during the summer.

Europe was great, but there were things about Europe that I did not like. I hated being thousands of miles from the people I loved most. I wasn't fond of the idea that my twenty-seven-year-old friends had to ask their parents for permission to stay out late, and I always wanted more than two ice cubes in my soft drink.

I lived in Greece, Italy, Russia, Israel, and South Korea. In fact, I traveled all across Europe, and it did not cost me a dime. Can you say blessed? My European life taught me to look for the best in others' differences instead of judging them because of those differences.

My first year in Italy was tough. I could not speak the language and did not live in a touristic city; very few people spoke English besides some of my teammates. During my second season playing in Italy, I got a new teammate who was studying English in college. I helped her with her English, and she helped me with my Italian. Because of my Spanish background, I picked up the Italian language pretty fast. There was a restaurant in the small town of Alessandria where I ate every game day. At first, I struggled with my food order and often ordered the wrong thing. I couldn't figure out if the owner enjoyed making me pay for the three meals I'd ordered before I got it right or if he just didn't like Americans.

Once I learned to speak, I walked in and ordered as though I was born and raised in *Italia*. After I placed my order, the sixty-year-old owner looked at me and said in beautiful English, "It's about time you learned to speak Italian." I couldn't believe this dude. He spoke English all along. We had a laugh about it and ended up becoming really good friends. He comped most of my meals after that. At that point, I decided that no matter where I ended up, I would try hard to adjust to the new culture and learn the new language. My new way of thinking was effective and helped me to win over a lot of people.

As Americans, we tend to expect people to speak our language. I made it a point to learn enough words in other countries to show that I was trying my best to blend in. I could never really speak Russian, Greek, Hebrew, or Korean, but I learned enough to at least understand the gist of conversations. Playing in Europe taught me how to depend on others as well as how to have faith in others. I learned that I had to trust people to help me get acclimated to my new environment. Dependence and trusting others had always been and will always be difficult for me.

The pros allowed me the luxury of a truly blessed life; however, I paid a high price for it. Because of my basketball career and the pitfalls that come with the pro lifestyle, I lost everything that was dear to me. I played in New York during the summers and in Europe in the winter. I saw my family and loved ones less than two months in ten years; they became almost strangers to me. It was as though I was putting my real life on pause to finish my current life. I literally allowed basketball to consume me, and I completely lost sight of who I was. I became basketball; I judged my self-worth on how well I performed. It was a type of obsessive sickness that cost me the most important things in life.

My basketball career has been full of great triumphs as well as great devastation. It seems crazy now to look back and see the way my basketball career brought the best and worst life had to offer right to my doorstep. However, my life and its shoes are the only ones I'd ever want to wear. Despite the circumstances, I can honestly say that, "my shoes will always be the best fit for me."

My career steps taught me that life is easier with money. Some people even view life as better with money, but money, accolades, and fame have little significance in the long run. In the end, the only thing that really matters is what lives in our hearts. If material things own your heart, then one day you will be sorely disappointed.

My professional career taught me one of the most valuable lessons I believe a person could ever learn. I learned that great leaders are the ones who are guided by a humble heart. Great leaders have the ability to genuinely relate to people from all walks of life because they truly realize that everyone is always one short step from both success and failure. Great leaders tend to place others first and themselves second. This may sound odd, but I truly feel that being a pro athlete taught me the importance of humility.

19

Choose Happiness

*"Success is not the key to happiness.
Happiness is the key to success."*

— *Albert Schweitzer*

Happiness is a strange anomaly to me. I spent my whole life seeking it, when in fact all I had to do was choose happiness. It is easier said than done. But happiness is a choice. In my past, I would get so caught up in my problems or the things I viewed as bad in my life that happiness seemed so far away. Most think happiness is a destination that they will eventually arrive at, when in fact happiness is something you choose. Happiness is not a destination. It doesn't have an end. It is a part of a journey. I just never realized that and thought I was just excluded from being happy.

Everyone sees being a pro athlete as a tropical

destination profession. However, few witness the hard work and sacrifice the athlete and their family concede for one another. I personally spent less than four months accumulated over my career with my family once I became a professional athlete. At the time, I was okay with being far away from my family. But then, one day, my dad unexpectedly passed away. It happened all too suddenly. My dad and I had not spoken for over six months when he reached out on my birthday and I didn't answer. Three days later, he passed away.

If I could change one moment in my life, I would have answered that call, but that's a whole different story. After his passing, my mom wasn't doing well, so I resigned from my job and moved home to be with her without a second thought. That was the first time I chose something over basketball. It made my mom happy because I'd been away for so long. Losing my father on bad terms left a hole in my heart.

At that time, I realized that my mom loved me in her own way. My grandma had all the time in the world to sit me on her lap and shower me with affection. My mom never did that. I thought that meant she didn't love me. But as an adult, I now realize that my mom just didn't have time and wasn't getting much help. She struggled to make ends meet, sometimes walking hours for food, and there was no time left to pat her kids on the head. Her love showed through the hardships she endured and the sacrifices she made for us. But as a kid, I didn't see that. As a kid, you just want what you want, even if what you want isn't what you need.

I decided to help coach kids in basketball while

I was home. Little did I know, that was exactly what the doctor ordered. The unconditional love I received from those students not only filled my cup back up, it brought so much joy and happiness into my life. I knew being with my mom would bring me happiness. I thought I was moving in with my mom to take care of her, when in fact, the amount of love the Divine One sent my way gave me the courage to really take the first steps towards self-love.

We have the ability to select which memories we allow to mold us. We have the right to choose which memories we allow to guide us. Why is it so easy for us to decide to cling to the bad ones? I think we subconsciously allow the bad memories to rule our lives because their trauma left a greater impact on our psyche. In some cases, we sometimes attempt to create new memories to bury the bad ones. It is where we make up the reality we wished for. I have been in both places. As a child, I made up stories about my family to cover up our truths and hide the hurt. I spent a lot of time in that space, often suffering in the non-reality of my lies. I just wanted to feel normal. I wanted to outrun the shame that I later learned was not mine to bear. Then, there was a time where I accepted my reality, only to later let society make me feel as though death was a better option.

As I grow as a person, I now look back on the good stories in my life. I decided I want the good feelings that accompany those stories to be my guiding light. The bad feelings have to find another place to call home. I will serve those bad feelings with an eviction notice so they can never dwell within me again.

I invite you to do the same. Take a leap of faith.

Make the decision to be the captain of your own ship. Quit allowing others, their indiscretions, your faults, and your demons to keep you from experiencing a life and a love that you are entitled to. We cannot choose all of the things and events that we encounter in life, whether good or bad, but we can choose how we let them affect us. Never allow yourself to marinate in the negatives life throws your way.

Sometimes we have to simply choose happiness. It is so easy to let ourselves get bogged down with bad feelings and dwell in the presence of misery. Negative feelings allow us to blame others and release ourselves from the task of taking responsibility for our own lives. Continuous negative feelings will rob us of the beautiful life God intended for us. It is our choice to stop it.

There are so many opportunities placed in our paths to help us overcome obstacles, achieve our greatest dreams, and become anything we set our minds on. We have to recognize the opportunities, be willing to step out of our comfort zones, and open our minds to other people and other things that do not necessarily fall within our idea of normal. I truly believe that our differences as people make each of us unique to God's plan.

Remember, happiness is always just around the corner from horror. Even though negative memories leave heavy scars that attempt to blot out positive memories, we have to focus on the good memories intently. Hopefully, they will override the bad ones. My life is filled with many wonderful memories, and these memories saved me from myself. They block out society's inability to accept me, and they continually point me in the right direction. I decide to walk in faith.

20

Looking Back

"A strong, positive self-image is the best possible preparation for success."

— Joyce Brothers

All of my life, I've tried very hard to understand and accept other people's differences instead of passing judgment on anyone. Each of us is a unique individual, born with major life differences and circumstances. Each of us behaves the way we do because of the experiences we've had, the obstacles we've faced, and how we chose to react to those situations.

Since each person's set of circumstances is so different, it makes it impossible to expect anyone to feel, act, or lead the same exact life as you. God gave us free will. Whether we choose right, wrong, or indifferent is for God to judge. God could have simply wrinkled his nose and made us all uniform in the way we think, live, and act, but He gifted us with free will. Why, then, does society feel the need to challenge that? For some reason, God believes in us. It is our society that sometimes does not.

I am not an expert Bible scholar. I am not my sexuality. In fact, my sexuality isn't even one percent of who I am as a person. I am just one person who has suffered numerous setbacks as well as faced and conquered many obstacles. I wrote this book to attempt to uplift other imperfect people like me. We all suffer setbacks. We all experience joy and pain. We all struggle to fight the demons in our lives. Through this book, I hope and pray that each reader will feel encouraged to make life changes. Take time to read and recognize God's signs to help guide you to find and follow your path. I hope that you learn to truly love yourself and others as God has loved us: without condition.

Life deals everyone hard blows. Some people's blows are much more difficult than others. It is up to us to find the strength to have the courage and determination to let those difficult things go. Holding on to brokenness is not good for the human spirit. Choosing happiness is your human right. But happiness cannot be achieved if you never release the pain. Forgiveness and forgetting have two completely different meanings. Forgiveness is letting go of the pain that people caused you. The trick is to always attempt to remember the lesson the pain taught you instead of constantly remembering the pain itself. Let go of the hurt and find your fate.

Hope is the foundation on which life is built. As long as you can hold on to even a sliver of hope, you can be what you want to be and excel in things that no one ever thought were possible for you to accomplish. This book is here to urge you to unload the excuses. Take ownership of your life and paint an enduring masterpiece. Stop being someone else's victim. Break the cycle you were born in. Dare to be different. Dare to not only dream, but strive with everything in you to make your dreams come true. Find yourself as only you can.

21

Leaving a Legacy

"The choices we make about the lives we live determine the kinds of legacies we leave."

— *Tavis Smiley*

As a coach, I feel as though I have the opportunity to affect lives and give back to others. I am blessed enough to be able to leave my legacy to young basketball players. I continuously ask myself if it's enough in comparison to all I have been given.

I now realize that we all leave a legacy. Some legacies are great, while others are minor. Some legacies impact a multitude of people, while others only impact a few. Legacies can be positive or negative. No matter what kind of life we lead, each of us leaves an imprint on the people around us. The entirety of our life's words and actions influence how others view us, and speak to who we are.

Both of my parents attended college, but I was the first in our family to graduate college. Graduating college was not only important for me and my life; it set a precedent of success for my younger siblings. The valor I showed to break the cycle gave my younger sisters and brother the courage to succeed. I exposed them to possibilities.

The legacy I started not only lives in them, but our children recognize success. They are aware of the difficult road ahead and how hard a person has to work to reach that destination. They understand that there might be potholes, detours, and that they may even run out of gas on their journey to success. They also understand that it only takes one person with a dream, who constantly displays guts and determination, to achieve overwhelming possibilities.

All of us must realize that our lives influence everyone around us. Even though most of the time, we have no idea who we are influencing. Our mere presence in life is influencing someone. Maybe it's a friend or maybe it's a kid who has a troubled home life, or maybe it's someone who lives by our examples. How we live our life can give others hope, the type of hope that cannot be found in anything in their immediate lives. Finding the moral courage to set good examples instead of bad ones is a must. It is truly a problem our society faces today. At present, the number of icons who endorse drinking, sex, disrespect of others, and living selfishly far outnumber people who actually parent their children.

Our youth idolize the wrong things. Simply put, they are misled. They *see* the glorified side of those things, but they often *experience* the bad side of those same things. Many of us think we are sheltering our children by not engaging them in conversations pertaining to drugs, sex, alcohol, and decision-making skills. We need to have these difficult discussions with our children and stress to them the need to surround themselves with the right kind of people at an early age. I would much prefer that my daughters hear those things from me than take advice about the pros and cons of those things from their peers.

I want my legacy and way of life to be imprinted in my children. I want them to be equipped for life's pitfalls by educating them on both the positives and the negatives of important issues. I want to give them a chance to make strong, wise decisions in this difficult world.

We lose sight of the fact that the world is constantly growing and changing. If we don't grow, change, and adapt as parents, our kids end up paying a heavy price. My mother couldn't raise me the way her mother raised her, and I can't raise my daughters the way my mother raised me.

Kids are learning the wrong things at a younger age. This is something we should admit and embrace instead of fight. We want our kids to be smarter quicker; we even pay coaches to help them become better athletes faster. Sorry to break it to you, but when we live in a society that pushes our youth to learn faster we also invite the learning of the harsher things life has to offer earlier. Since I can't raise my children in a bubble atmosphere, educating them about the perils of life to the best of my abilities is my only weapon. Even though I won't raise my kids exactly the way my mom raised me, I can instill in them the core values that some children are missing today. I just have to find a way to teach it in a language they buy into and understand.

Long gone are the days where children did or didn't do things just because their parents told them to or not to. Educating your children about sex, drugs, and alcohol doesn't mean that you are giving them your permission to run right out and do them. Eventually, we have to decide what we as parents can live with. Our children's innocence is being invaded from every angle. My children will definitely understand the pitfalls of activities that so many people today make out to be nothing more than fun times. Innocent enough, right? I can promise you, there is nothing fun or innocent about being a drug addict, alcoholic, raising a child at thirteen, or living on the street. I would rather discuss the uncomfortable things at an earlier age than deal with the consequences of allowing my kids to learn them from someone else.

What will be your legacy? Will you choose to leave something positive with everyone you meet? I don't want to be remembered as just a great basketball player. I want people to remember me for how I made them feel when they were around me; how I often encouraged them to revisit some of their thought processes and how I brought moments of joy and wisdom into their lives. God did not bless me with so many peaks and valleys, good and bad times, positive and negative experiences to keep them to myself. As I noted earlier, I truly believe that "to whom much is given, much is expected."

FINDING MYSELF

I have spent my whole life searching for myself. The more time I spend searching, the more I realize that all I have to do is look at my brothers and sisters, children, players, and friends. My legacy can be found alive and well in their actions and hearts. I find myself not in my shortcomings and not in the basketball record books, but I find myself every day in the lives I've affected.

22

Reflections

"Do not judge me by my successes, judge me by how many times I fell down and got back up."

— *Nelson Mandela*

I've written down my feelings throughout my life because I felt as though I had no one to talk to. I've sometimes struggled to communicate my feelings verbally, so I've always written about my emotions. In fact, I still continue to feel that I express myself more clearly in my writings. Some of my written words are in the form of poems and some are writings reflecting on a moment that deeply affected me.

I share my stories and experiences with you because I want you to understand my thought processes during certain times in my life and witness some of the ups and downs that I have gone through. Even though I'm living a life most see in a glorified way, I still have many dark days. No one is exempt from life's satire. This, to me, is what makes us all equal.

Life doesn't see color or social class, and it doesn't play favorites to privilege. We are all on a turbulent journey to become the best versions of ourselves, something that probably could not happen if things were always perfect in our lives. For some reason, pain seems to be one of our most ruling lessons. People who haven't experienced tough times usually have difficulties being empathetic to others. I'm citing this to say that hard times don't last; difficult times turn us into strong people who not only last but thrive in the face of adversity. Enjoy my writings; may they bring you soul searching and peace.

When your soul feels broken
Wondering if it can be fixed
Obsessed with dying
Praying, hoping my time will come quick
When others look at me, I never see what they see
An empty barren soul resides inside of me
I know the Lord doesn't make mistakes
He keeps waiting on me patiently
I live the best I can, however imperfectly
Doubt and fear, the biggest enemy of mankind
They flow through my soul and heart
They have taken over my mind
Every failure and disappointment forever locked in my head
Praying for it to all end
Beyond ready to escape this dread

When your heart is blind
Your eyes can't see
Blinded from everything that's meant to be
I refuse to submit to this pain
Moving on even if it drives me insane
Can't make you love all that is me
I'll live in this place
I guess that's how it's meant to be

With you I feel free
Free to be me
However imperfect I may be
You see me for me

Photographic memory of your touch, your kiss, your smile
Your ways haunt me daily
Forget you, never, that will take a while
You provoke my pain
Somedays it feels like a hundred days standing in the rain
Pictures of you and me
Burnt forever in my memory
I hope and pray there is someone out there for me
Dope enough to erase you from my memory
You raped my trust by supporting my love habit
Only fools believe in love you silly rabbit

My beautiful friend
Where do I begin?
I'll start with this
I miss your sensual kiss
Soul searching, finding my way through
All paths, all roads wind right back to you
Your smile, everything you do
Even the annoying things keep me falling off the cliff for you
From A to Z
All that matters is I got you and you got me
If you could hear my heart and see my soul
You would undoubtedly know

You and me, me and you
Everyday through and through
You teach me and I'll teach you
Worlds apart, but giving our just due
When it ends, no one will know
We watered our love with pain
And that shit made it grow
Accepting imperfections got us through
It will always be
You for me and me for you

Time is brutally wise
It reveals all things we try to hide
They say it's a gift and a curse to hear your inner voice with
great clarity
It rapes my inner peace along with my sincerity
Father Time I respectfully respect thee
Time catches up to you repeatedly

Everytime I think of you
My heart still can't believe it's true
You were taken from us way too soon
Your smile made everyone feel like they could walk on the moon
Missing you is something I'll do everyday
Still confused why you were taken that way
I guess it's something we will never understand
By faith, I'll choose to believe it all part of God's masterplan
All I know is, I can't wait to see you again
Even though it means this life has to end

R.I.P. Eric Tremayne Smith

Sometimes there is a love that transcends all things
Not space, nor time, not even obstacles can stop this all
consuming thing
Even though you're there and I'm here
No distance is enough to quench this thirst I fear
We have become two different people with two different lives
But this rapture we share took on its own life, It's alive
Technically you're his not mine
But try telling that to two hearts that stayed connected through
distance and time
You're the flesh of my flesh, heart of my heart
The longing and aching of my soul will never let us be far apart
I love that you're happy and love is always near
For when you truly love their happiness is like beautiful words
whispered in an ear

NightMares

Avoiding sleep over and over again
When I close my eyes the reality of my nightmares begin
Two hearts so beaten and battered all the way through
In my dream, she loves me the way I want her to
Soul searching with every beat of my heart
Has taught me that real love is truly a dead art
Desperately wanting her to see me for who I am really am
But to an aloof heart, my love is just another man scam
Desolation and grief have bonded together my pain
Praying for the love of a woman full of unfiltered disdain
At the end of a dream, I don't want to see come true
Learning to live with a piece of my soul belonging to you

When times get hard
When life seems tough
Our real friends wade in the trenches with us
They willingly share in our pain
They help us navigate through storms and rain
I guess I'm saying thanks for being you
Thanks for being steadfast and true

Similar souls traveling different roads
Different journeys, completely different ties
I fell off the cliff the moment I looked into your eyes
With dreams and hopes of making you mine
Two restless souls with hearts that can't quite align
Souls ragged and torn from life's riptide
Dreaming, sailing, searching, floating
Two brave hearts collide
I was lost inside until I found you
You filled me with hope
It was like there was nothing I couldn't do
Except earn your love or get through to you

You fill up my empty space
All wrongs become rights
I see a better me every second you're in my life
If you could see my heart through a microscopic lens
You'd see that your love consumes every fiber of me within
If you'd let down your walls and share this space with me
Good is an enemy of great
Forget about good and come be great with me

I keep you alive in my heart
Your smile is never far from my thoughts
I try so hard not to question God's plan
But this is so hard to understand
Your family misses you and loves you even more in death
The ache in my heart sometimes leaves me holding my breath
I spend quality time with my pain
I take it everywhere, it occupies my brain
I'm learning to thrive with emptiness in my chest
The old me died
Just can't put this feeling to rest

R.I.P Billy Wayne Robinson

Captured by a love I'm not sure exist
Prisoner to slave how did it get like this
I scale the walls and see my freedom
In your eyes and smile are the keys to my kingdom
As a moth is drawn to a flame and burned by the fire
I return to your love, what bitter, sweet satire
You play with my heart and your lips command my emotions
You play it so well, you have my full devotion

In this transition
Trying to find my way
Longing for your love everyday
All my fears and doubts are outside my door ready for war
I keep trying to take what's lost and broken and make a new start
Asking myself, why don't they make medicine for a broken
heart?

Getting my footing
Finding Myself
Didn't think I'd make it after you left
Sleepless nights and my days have changed
Nothing will ever erase you cause you're in my veins
I close my eyes and see your smile
I'd fight lions and tigers and bears
I'd run a thousand miles
I search myself and all I see are remnants of you
My smile, my walk all the way to my thoughts are just like you
You'll always be my guy, my guy in the sky

R.I.P. Billy Wayne Robinson

It's the crackle of the candle
The feel of your skin
The way you kiss me
Where do I begin
The taste of your lips
The way you move is everything
I could never forget
I want you
No, I need you
Never want this feeling to end

Wanting something so bad, it's hard to live
It's like living a million lives in a couple of years
This is the kind of love that can make you go mad
Feels like you're living at the depths of sad
They say between what is said and not meant
And what is meant and not said
Most love is lost
I'm still trying to hold on to you at all cost

Perfect love drives out fear
I guess that's why I feel like someone else when you're near
Love is my superpower
When I'm with you, mine grows hour by hour
I'll love you till forever ends
This euphoria has my whole life in a tailspin.

How many times can a person die inside without killing
their soul?
Hallucinations of a love so pure
Forces at play I've never felt before
I feel you like sweet melodies touch the soul
The deep warmth of love, but still so cold
Fantasies of the unknown has me changing gears
Chasing you, forgetting all fears
Two souls colliding totally out of control
Still, your love caresses my soul
Entangled to the bittersweet end with the truth
She can't seem to love the same way I do.

They say patience in love protects the heart
Heart beating fast, the suspense is tearing me apart
Dove into this love with no inhibitions
Trying to survive my own emotional prison
In servitude to this love, my heart beats for her
I know I found my dream in you
Knowing we are made by the struggles we choose
She is mine part one and two
I'd walk an eternity in another life searching for you.

We parallel in so many ways
From the kind of women we chose to love
Down to the kids we chose to raise
Your talent became mine
I see you in me over space and time
You gave up your life for me
That trait is alive residing in me

R.I.P Billy Wayne Robinson

The Legacy of Crystal Robinson

Here's what some of those influenced by Crystal Robinson have to say about her legacy:

KIRSTY COOK

"In life, things happen that will either define us or make us stronger." Crystal told me that once, and since then, I have used that as a motto for my life. Coming back to the basketball team eight months pregnant my senior year with a brand new coach was scary. She didn't know me, and I didn't know her. She could have looked at me and simply made a decision that I was nothing, right then and there, which was what I was expecting (the worst). Being pregnant in high school is not an easy task, but with a lot of support, it can be done successfully. Believe me, I know. Crystal never judged me or looked down on me; instead, she lifted me up and believed in me when I felt like no one else did.

There are certain people God places in your life

to teach you a lesson, and there are certain people whom He places at the perfect times to stay for good. Honestly, I'm not sure if I would have made it through high school without the help I received from Crystal Robinson. She stayed on me hard, and at times, I felt like she was pushing me so hard that it might be impossible to do the things she wanted. But she never set goals for me that she knew I couldn't complete. One time I told her, "I can't do it!" and she looked at me with this blank face and said, "You know what my momma used to tell me, and I'm about to tell you, 'One time can whooped ole can't's ass until it could.'" Needless to say, I tried to refrain from telling Crystal that I couldn't do something.

The greatest thing about Crystal is that she is so loyal. I know that if I ever needed anything from the smallest to the largest task she would be there. She stood by us even when we were being downed and called the underdogs. She made sure to tell us every day how much she believed in us and how much she knew that we could do it. Crystal is someone I look up to and I think she can be depended on to be a role model for kids and people in general everywhere.

She definitely helped change my life for the better and taught me to never give up because people are going to knock you down, but it's up to you to get back up. She taught me that sometimes silence is your best friend, and she's the only person in my whole entire life that I can say I have ever been scared of.

During a game once I messed up so bad and I knew she was so mad and I could hear her screaming my name to come over to the bench. But I ignored her, and when the last seconds ran off the clock, I knew something was about to happen because I could just hear her talking to the assistants and slamming things around. At one point I heard her say to the ref, "Can I throw a shoe at one of my own players?" When it was time to shake hands, I skipped all that and went straight to the dressing room, so I wouldn't have to go over there by her because I knew I was about to get the chewing of my life. That was probably one of the top five scariest moments of my life. When we got in the dressing room that's exactly what happened.

When she's in the zone, she means business. One of the best things about Crystal is how passionate she is, not just about basketball but about life in general. She taught me that if I'm going to do something, to do it a hundred percent, and to leave it all on the floor.

Crystal is truly one of the greatest people I have ever met. She is one of the kindest people I have ever known. She will help anyone who needs it, never expects anything in return, and is always ready to lend a hand when someone asks. She is trustworthy and down to earth. She taught me that choices are made by you, and you only, and that you are the person that controls your life. She taught me to never be ashamed of where you came from because the mistakes and accomplishments you have done make you who you are. She taught me that self-control is usually best and that there are certain times for certain things. She has affected my life in more ways than I can count and stood beside me and helped me when I felt like I only had a few people on my team.

She has truly been one of the most influential people in my life and still is day to day.

She still rides me to do the right things and make the right decisions, and I know that when I need her, she will be there, ready to help. She has encouraged me and helped me, and she will forever be a role model and life-long friend. She is absolutely one of the greatest people I have ever known, and I'm so blessed and thankful she is part of my life.

CHARITY HULL

As a young girl growing up and playing basketball in southeastern Oklahoma, I wanted to be like one person: Crystal Robinson. She was a legend in girls' basketball, and as I grew older, I followed her collegiate career and eventually her career in the WNBA. In July 2009, I began my teaching and coaching career with McAlester Public Schools in McAlester, Oklahoma. One day in late July or early August 2009, I was in the cafeteria at McAlester High School helping with the paperwork for junior high and high school girls' physicals. The high school principal at the time, Randy Hughes, came up to me with a *huge* smile on his face and told me that they had hired a new varsity girls' basketball coach, Crystal Robinson. The first thought I had was, "Okay, so who is this lady?" Not because I didn't recognize the name, but because I assumed that the Crystal Robinson McAlester High School had hired to coach girls' basketball wasn't *the* Crystal Robinson. Luckily, I had assumed incorrectly, and the Crystal Robinson that McAlester had somehow managed to hire was *the* Crystal Robinson.

The first time I met Crystal, a few days later, at the

new teacher induction, I was far more impressed by meeting her than she was by meeting me, one of her future assistants. At the new teacher induction that first morning, all thirty-six of the newly hired teachers had to go around and introduce themselves. Crystal was asked to go first and of course obliged. After listening to her speak about herself, I had two thoughts: I was impressed with the person she was, and I felt sorry for the person who had to follow her. Well as it turned out that person was me. I don't remember what I said, and that isn't important. But what is important is that a few months later, Crystal said to me that what I said that day made an impression on her and that at that moment she was looking forward to working with me.

Coaching with Crystal was intimidating for me as a young, new coach. I was starting my career as an assistant coach to the greatest female basketball player to ever play in Oklahoma, I knew I was in over my head and I knew that I was going to be a disappointment to her. She would expect me to be a brilliant basketball mind, and I knew that she had forgotten more about basketball than I had ever known in my life. But that wasn't the case. Crystal accepted me, with my limited basketball knowledge and all. She saw my strengths and used them to her advantage and the teams' advantage and together, along with our team, we had success. To say that working with Crystal has changed my life is cliché, but it is true. I have learned so much from her.

Yes, of course, my knowledge of basketball has increased exponentially, but basketball is the area she has influenced me the least. Over the course of the year we worked together it seems that it would be easy to see the greatest accomplishment we made: we won a state championship... Okay, let's be honest, she and the girls won a state championship, I was just blessed enough and lucky enough to be along for the ride. But what I learned in the year I worked alongside Crystal and in the years we have remained friends reaches far beyond the basketball court and the gym. I learned to always surround myself with people who excel at what they do.

It is said that we become like the five people we spend the most time with, so surround yourself with people you want to be like. Crystal is one of those people. She taught me to never be afraid to want something and to go after it; if it weren't for Crystal I probably wouldn't be pursuing my Master's degree. Before I met Crystal, I always cared what other people thought of me, or I should say I cared too much what people thought of me. I placed most of my self-worth in the opinions of others. Crystal taught me to value me for me. If people can't accept who I am, flaws and all, then they don't deserve me. Know your strengths and use them to help you succeed. Know your weaknesses and surround yourself with people who have those strengths. Never be afraid to ask for help. Accept nothing less than the best from people. Set the bar high. You only get what you expect from people.

I witnessed firsthand Crystal take a team of high school girls, a team who the previous season had lost their best player to graduation and had lost their coach to the collegiate level, and win a state championship. This was a team with exponentially more heart than talent. Oh, the talent was there, in the form of a sophomore guard and freshman guard, but this was a team that was a hundred and ten percent heart. Crystal believed in them and they believed in her. She was clear in her expectations of them and when they reached or exceeded these expectations they were rewarded, but when they failed to reach these expectations, there were consequences. I could probably write my own book of Crystal Robinson stories, but I won't continue with the anecdotes. I will conclude with this: many of the people that I have met that know I know Crystal often want to ask questions about her that relate to her time as player and coach, and while her accomplishments on the court are noteworthy and astonishing, I would much rather tell you about Crystal, my friend.

Jenni McMurray

The best type of friend to have is the kind that makes you a better person. Whether they mean to change you or if it's just a side effect of your friendship, it is instrumental in who you are today. I have had the pleasure of having great friends, but one friend in particular comes to mind when I think of who has affected me, helped me grow and become confident in my role. Because of the opportunity I had to work with Crystal I have become a better person, a more confident person. Much of what I owe Crystal isn't in what she said, but in how she treated me and made me feel like I belonged.

The year I worked as Crystal's assistant, I learned so much about the game of basketball. Her knowledge of the game is astounding. She has played in countless games and has seen nearly every circumstance and that makes her prepared for an infinite number of situations. By observing her on the sideline I see the game differently. I see the strengths and weaknesses of the other team as well as their tendencies. It seems as though Crystal can see the game unfold before it has happened. Since working with her, I can predict the outcome of some situations during a game. And when it seems that there is nothing that can be done, Crystal always seems to have something in her back pocket. I use the knowledge I gained during my time with Crystal to help me coach my junior varsity team. The confidence Crystal places in her team is something I try to instill in my team. You don't have to be the best, but you have to work hard and execute, by doing the little things right. By being confident in doing the little things, you set yourself up for success. Small victories equal big wins eventually.

I hope that I can have a lasting effect on someone like Crystal has had on me. She inspires me personally and professionally because she doesn't try to be something she isn't. Before I became acquainted with Crystal I knew of her as a stellar athlete, but as a person, Crystal is Crystal no matter where she is or who she is around. It is refreshing to know there are people who are "real" in this superficial world we live in. The confidence she exudes is contagious. She expects to be successful in everything she does. Crystal has been an assistant before and she knows what the role of an assistant coach is. She set a high standard for how a head coach should treat an assistant coach. She helped me to become confident in my role as an assistant coach. She was gracious and kind in the learning curve of a first-time coach. She helped me navigate the obstacles that come with being a counselor, a nurse, a secretary, a taxi driver, a lost-and-found, and countless other jobs that are typically fulfilled by an assistant.

It's hard to put into words how much of an affect Crystal has had on my life. She taught me the importance of having a goal and doing whatever it takes to make that goal a reality. In the time I've known Crystal, I have become more and more amazed at the person she is. She is compassionate and caring, determined and strong willed, competitive and motivating. She possesses character traits that not only make her an amazing coach but an amazing person and friend. A quote by Henry Brooks Adams sums up how Crystal has influenced my life: "A teacher affects eternity; he can never tell where his influence stops."

KAYLIE BAXTER

When I made the decision to pursue a collegiate career in basketball at Murray State College for Coach Crystal Robinson, I was incredibly excited and anxious. My father was involved with Southeastern Oklahoma State University athletics, and I grew up watching Crystal play. I envied her talents and wished that someday I could be a college basketball star like she was. This was my dream and to see it finally become a reality meant an incredible amount to me, especially when I had been blessed with the opportunity to play for someone who has had so much success as a player and a coach. When I signed my letter of intent in April 2012, many people doubted my abilities and discouraged my pursuit of a collegiate basketball career. Sometimes it seemed like my closest friends and family were the only ones who believed in me. "You're not quick enough" or "You'll never be able to compete at that level" were just a couple of the things I heard on a weekly basis. With these opinions racing through my head, my confidence in myself began to decline. I started to worry and wonder if these things were actually true. Thoughts like, "Maybe I'm making a mistake... Maybe I'm not good enough," began to soar through my mind, but this all changed on August 13, 2012.

August 13, 2012 was a day that would change my life forever. This was our reporting day for basketball at Murray State College. This was the day I had so anxiously longed for. This was the day that would lead me to become the person I am today. As I began to pack my things into the car and prepare for the big move, butterflies arose inside me. The thoughts and assumptions of others began to pile back into my worrying brain. I knew what I was doing was right, and this was exactly where God wanted me to be, so I pushed all the negative thoughts to the back of my mind and began thinking positively. After all, I couldn't look like a nervous wreck for my first impression on my new teammates. The first couple of days brought sadness, happiness, and of course, a new beginning. On reporting day, we had to weigh in. You know, most girls do not like the scale, and I fit into that category. I had not been on a scale in over four months. I weighed in at 173.2 pounds. This was the most I had ever weighed. I was so angry at what I let myself become over the summer. When Coach

Robinson walked over to me and saw my weight, she said, "You are going to have to lose at least fifteen pounds to be competitive at this level." The look on my face, I'm sure, was priceless as thoughts like these ran through my head, "Fifteen pounds! I have never lost even five pounds in my life, how am I going to lose fifteen?"

As the weeks went on, our workouts started to become more vigorous and some days I thought there was no way I was going to make it out alive, but I did. Although playing for Coach Robinson was fun and beneficial, it was not always rainbows and butterflies. The workouts were difficult and the saying, "Only the strong survive," applies perfectly. For example, when we began the 2012–13 school year, we had fourteen girls, and when the season ended, eight of us were still representing Murray State Lady Aggies basketball. Coach Robinson is a fiery, compassionate, and competitive person that gets into every play of every game. She demands your best effort all the time, and some people were just not cut out for her style of coaching. She always had high expectations and wanted us to push ourselves, because she could see the potential inside us. That was one of the first things I learned from Coach Robinson. "If you want to be the best you have to be willing to put in the work that the best requires." Growing up with both my parents being coaches, I was destined to be competitive, and that I am. When she would say these words, I would push myself to limits I had no idea I could reach. Limits like weighing in at 155.4 pounds after only a couple months of hard work. The scale wasn't the only place where I could see changes in myself. I could see myself changing not only physically but mentally and emotionally as well.

One of my biggest struggles was my mental game. This is a part of my game I would say Coach Robinson has affected me the most. "Get that look off your face," these were words I heard often throughout this season from her. Most of the time I heard those words when I had just missed a makeable shot or made a mistake on defense. I would get so down on myself that I would mentally take myself out of the game, but Coach Robinson was always there to provide that little boost of confidence I needed to go back in there and hit a big shot, get a steal, or grab some boards. Throughout our season she would call on me in crucial moments of the game to knock down a shot even if I hadn't had the best shooting night. The confidence she had in me made me believe in myself. When I missed a shot she would say, "Keep shooting, you've got the next one!" And when I passed up an open shot, I would look over at the bench and see that wide-eyed look that meant, "If you don't shoot the ball I am going to sit you right beside me." Coach Robinson saw past my flaws and setbacks and believed that I could become great.

Although being a great basketball player is a profound achievement, it wasn't Coach Robinson's most important goal for my teammates and me. She encouraged us and taught each of us throughout this year how to become better people all around. My teammates and I were not allowed to miss class or be late. This was a part of her plan to show us that we are student athletes. Coach Robinson wanted us to see how being prompt and respectful could benefit us in numerous ways. She was adamant on showing us that basketball is a gateway to multiple opportunities much greater than most people imagine. "No one believed I could, and that's why I did." I remember hearing these words often in our pre-practice or pregame huddles. Coach Robinson wanted us to dream, to realize that in basketball or any aspect of life we could be anything we want to be if we were willing to work at it. She also wanted us to take advantage of every moment we have with our fellow teammates. She strived to teach us that being a team means being a family. Not only on the court, but off it as well.

If I were to write down everything Coach Robinson has taught me that year, I would be writing a never-ending book, but the few things I have listed are just some highlights of my year with her. Crystal Robinson is more than just a great coach, or an incredible athlete back in the day. She is a competitive, caring, and compassionate leader who loves the game of basketball. My story is just one that she has affected, and I know there will be many more to come. I am Kaylie Baxter, and my decision to play under Crystal Robinson was one of the best decisions of my life.

DETARA LOFTON

In the three years that I have known Coach Crystal Robinson, I have never met a more genuine and loving individual. I don't know many people with a heart as genuine and unselfish as hers. Crystal Robinson has influenced my life more than she will ever know. I had the pleasure of meeting her through a friend of mine, who was her basketball manager. After just our first conversation, I knew that Coach Crystal was sent by God to be a major part of my life. She has been a tremendous help and support system for me. I can always count on her to help with anything that I need, and sometimes even things I would like to have but do not necessarily need. One of my favorite sayings of hers is, "I help those who help me," and that is a saying that she honors time and time again.

I have had the pleasure of having Crystal as a teacher but also as a coach. She bends over backwards to make sure that I have anything that my heart could desire. As a teacher, she has instilled a positive work ethic into me, which focuses me to push myself harder and be the great student that I know I can be. Her passion to improve people's individual talents and abilities is tremendous, I have never seen someone so driven to make others see what she sees in them. The fact that there is someone who cares so deeply for others is just remarkable to me. I would not have wanted to be a manager for any other coach than Crystal Robinson. Having known her has opened so many doors of opportunities for me that I could not have dreamed existed until now. I have been given the opportunity to further my education at a college, something that was out of reach before. She has made sure that all my needs regarding school and funding have been taken care of. I do not know many people who would do that for someone that they barely know, but Coach Crystal is doing it for me.

Things that I can take away from knowing Crystal

Robinson is that as long as you try, then you can succeed at anything that you put your mind to, the sky's the limit for my talents and abilities, and to never give up because despite any obstacle set before me I can achieve anything.

LESLEY HUFF

When my high school basketball coach called me two weeks before the start of my senior year to tell me that he was resigning to take another job, I immediately became devastated, and the tears began to flow uncontrollably. The only thing running through my head was that school started in two weeks, we had no coach, and the chances of a decent or average coach being hired this late in the game was slim to none. Little did I know, decent or average would not come close to describing the type of coach, better yet, the type of person that would be hired as the new basketball coach.

Growing up as a competitor and fan of basketball in Oklahoma, it was inevitable to hear about Crystal Robinson and her success and achievements. So you can imagine my surprise when the TV Productions teacher and Stringtown native pulled me aside while picking up my class schedule to inform me that there was a strong chance Crystal Robinson was going to become the new coach. It seemed too good to be true that someone with such experience and basketball knowledge would take a job in McAlester, coaching a team of girls she had never met nor seen play before, but that is exactly what happened.

Although I knew Crystal would contribute to the world of basketball for me in many ways, I could not have predicted the influence she would have on my life outside of the gym. When we were in the gym, we were all business; we focused on communication, teamwork, leadership, work ethic, and many other aspects of the game. Through example and explanation, she taught me the importance of understanding that every person is different, and therefore, you cannot approach all people the same way and expect the same response. She also taught me how true leaders operate. Rather than just giving directions to the people around them, the most important factor in being a good leader is leading by example, holding yourself accountable, and teaching others to hold themselves accountable. Crystal also taught me how to have hope in times that seem hopeless and how to persevere and triumph through adversity. One of the most memorable things she taught us was the importance of loyalty. All of this was something I initially learned on the court, but Crystal later reinforced and exemplified all of these things off the court as well.

As much as she taught me about basketball and the strategies, practices, and theories that go along with the sport, she has taught me even more about life off the floor. She has taught me things and helped guide me in ways that have made me a better person and pushed me in ways that continue to help me on the path to achieving my full potential in all aspects of life.

One of the most valuable things she has taught me was to remember where you came from and who has been by your side through the good and the bad. Whenever you come from a small town and one day attain stardom, it is very easy to leave the people from the beginning of your life behind, but Crystal was not one to do this. Rather than leaving the people of her past behind, she would always make an effort to help uplift them and encourage them to achieve success. Although I have always been one to want to help others, she has shown me the ways I can help the people around me, whether it be by doing something big or small.

Crystal exemplifies that you have the choice on whether you will or will not be the product of your environment. She could have very easily taken a path down the wrong road, but she made the decision to persevere through the trials and tribulations of life and decide that success was the only option. This has inspired me and truly made me a believer of the fact that you can achieve anything you set your mind to. This has also been an inspiration for me to help instill this same way of thinking to the students and athletes that I cross paths with as an educator and coach.

From the first time I met Crystal, I noticed that she is a person who is very proactive and confronts problems and issues head on. She has always been one to go to the source of the issue and confront it immediately rather than ignore it and let it build into something much bigger. By doing this, she not only ends the problem at hand, but she also demonstrates that she is not someone to be taken lightly or that you can take advantage of. In my eyes, this is a quality that portrays courage and strength, and therefore, it was a quality that I immediately began practicing in my daily life.

In addition, she has taught me the true meaning

of loyalty. I have seen her stand up against things whenever she feels they were unfair and unjust. She has shown me that loyalty is not only about being true to people when you are around them, it is also about defending and protecting them by all means necessary whether or not they are present. Her influence in just this area of my life has been observable for quite some time now. I have become a person who actively takes a stand whenever I feel as if someone is being mistreated, taken advantage of, or done wrong in any way. This has made me stronger in all aspects of my life and is something that I am forever grateful for.

The influence Crystal has had on my life up to this point cannot be done justice simply through explanation. It is something so significant that it can be observed in my day-to-day life. She has encouraged me, introduced me to many different people and opportunities, and taught me many different things I can utilize to help me succeed in the world today. She is completely honest and blunt with me about her opinions on the situations and decisions that I make in my life; she provided me with guidance on some of the most important decisions that I have made up to this point, and I can honestly say that she has never steered me wrong. Crystal has become more than just an inspiration and positive influence on my life. Above all else, she has become family to me.

APRIL PHILLIPS
Being the mom of four special needs children you prepare yourself for questions, stares, and

discrimination, but when I moved to Atoka, Oklahoma, I was not prepared for the love and acceptance my children received from Crystal Robinson. I still have the note she sent home with my son from school offering to help in any way because she saw the greatness within him and wanted to mentor him. I know my children will have to overcome many obstacles in life that others don't have to face, but no matter how hard life impacts them they will always have a champion cheering for them. Crystal saw past my children's disabilities and loved their abilities. It warmed my heart as my kids sat in their counseling session and when asked what was the best thing about moving to Atoka, both of the boys answered, "Meeting Coach Robinson."

Acknowledgements

I guess you could say I had big dreams for a kid from Stringtown, Oklahoma, population four-hundred-something. I wanted to play in the NBA, but there was no women's league at the time, so I looked up to guys. I hooped with all my male cousins and soon emerged as one of the best among them and there were some pretty damn good players that no one has ever heard about. I was one of the few girls playing baseball and basketball with the guys and competing at a high level. It was the one place I felt in control.

In hindsight, I can't believe I grew up in a town that is still twenty years behind time. I also can't believe it when my phone rings and it's someone who got my number, I'm not sure where, why or how, and most of the time, they need a favor, or for me to connect them to someone else. I mean people way bigger than the basketball world. So it's extremely hard for me to understand how people outside of basketball in the business world can find value in my skill set, but I'm still begging for validation from a basketball world I've been nothing but successful in. It is insulting to sit in an interview with someone when you have fifteen more years of experience than them, and you've played for or won a championship everywhere you've been, to be asked if you feel you are qualified for a job you've prepared your entire life for.

Like, for real, can this be my life? Well of course it is, now what does this mean? Trust the Universe? Basketball has been a great vessel, but it has never defined me.

And just like that, I walked away from the rat race, the search for validation, the desire to continue to prove I'm great. In all my years in basketball, I have few friends from that world, and the friends I did make, like Jessie Kenlaw and Raegan Pebley, have helped guide me, as well as talk me off a few ledges.

I can't wait to see what life has in store for me. I don't know much, but I can tell you this: all the struggles and ups and downs have equipped me with the necessary tools to handle whatever comes my way. I guess you can say it's freeing to let go of a need for validation and to live in your purpose.

I always felt like a fish out of water in the basketball world. I feel like I'm rare. I relate to straight shooters, or should I say, I trust people who are blatantly honest. Honesty is neutral for me. It doesn't offend for the most part. For me, greatness knows empathy on a deep level, and circumstances have usually taught to the greats that emotional intelligence and constructive criticism are vital to growth and they can be your greatest allies.

To my family: We have never been a perfect family,

but we have loved one another with unconditional hearts. We have always been there for each other during times of need. I am blessed to have been born into this family with all its imperfections.

To my first grade teacher Patty Harris: Thank you for looking at me and seeing the endless possibilities in me during a time when it wasn't considered the popular thing to do. Superheroes without capes make the world a tolerable place for all.

To my best friend Marvin: We made it to the other side just like we pinky swore we would as kids. You have been my best friend for what seems like an eternity. Even though we don't speak every day, we will forever be connected like night is to day.

To the Cochran family: Thank you for the many wonderful life lessons I learned through our friendship. Cindy, you are truly an angel amongst us. Thanks for your continued unconditional friendship. You'll always be near my heart.

To Jan Hargrave: You are truly one of the world's treasures, not because of your unique ability, but because of your heart for people. Thanks for your valuable contribution to my book, and even more so, for your undying friendship.

A school picture of Marvin.
"He looked like one of those bobblehead dolls."

Left to right: my cousin Mick and my sister B.J. in front of our house in Stringtown.

Left to right: my siblings Gerald, Billie and Brandi.

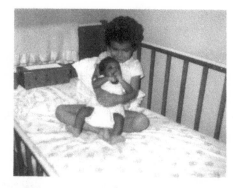

My brother Craig holding me, in our home in Stringtown.

Left to right: Craig and me, in our home in Stringtown.

Me and my friends at our church in Stringtown on Easter.
One of the the only pictures you'll ever see of me in a dress.

Left to right: Me and Craig, at our house in Stringtown.

CRYSTAL ROBINSON was born on January 22, 1974. In 1992, she was named a High School All-American by the Women's Basketball Coaches Association (WBCA). She participated in the inaugural WBCA High School Kodak All-American Game, scoring a game-high twenty-five points, and earning MVP honors. She attended Southeastern Oklahoma State University and was inducted into the NAIA Hall of Fame of Women's Basketball on March 18, 2003. Chosen to the *Daily Oklahoman* All-Century Team for both Oklahoma high schools and universities, she became just the third women's basketball player to be honored by the Association. After playing for the Colorado Xplosion in the American Basketball League, Robinson was selected as the sixth overall pick in the 1999 WNBA draft and played seven years for the New York Liberty. Robinson signed with the WNBA Washington Mystics on February 8, 2006 and then announced her retirement as a player the following year to become an assistant coach with the Mystics. Crystal became the first and only black woman ever inducted into the Oklahoma Sports Hall of Fame.